T0036461

Advance Praise for
THE ART OF BEING BROKEN

"My friend Kevin Hines has written a book that he is uniquely qualified to write. *The Art of Being Broken* is his true-life tale of searching the darkness to find the light, and it provides remarkable lessons for all of us. His personal story is harrowing, but the lessons are profound, including the techniques that ultimately helped him deal with his own suicidal thinking and ideation. To know Kevin is to know his motto: #BeHereTomorrow. It is at once both simple and powerful. There is no better messenger than Kevin Hines to inspire us to do just that."

—**Dr. Sanjay Gupta**, Chief Medical Correspondent, CNN

"*The Art of Being Broken: How Storytelling Saves Lives* is a powerful and deeply impactful look into the darkness that surrounds what Kevin Hines calls brain pain, a.k.a. mental illness. In this book, Kevin breaks down his story from the time his last book, *Cracked Not Broken*, ended until now. It remains a harrowing journey of true triumph over adversity. Kevin declares that he is not healed or cured, but remains in recovery and now utilizes transcendental meditation and other techniques he describes in the book to help keep him on an even keel. This book is meant for anyone going through pain right now, and reading it will surely help them find hope, healing, and overall wellbeing."

—**Bob Roth**, CEO of the David Lynch Foundation

"I met Kevin Hines when he was just a young man, not too long after his fateful leap off the Golden Gate Bridge. At the time, he was still finding himself, learning just who he was, what his survival meant and how he could use that knowledge to help others who might face the same impulse. Twenty years later, Kevin has evolved into one of the most forceful speakers and written on the subject of mental health. Still struggling with his own demons he nonetheless is on the front lines of his generation and others, coaching his coping mechanisms on how to survive a life that is not always kind. His latest book, *The Art of Being Broken: How Storytelling Saves Lives*, is merely the latest step that Kevin has made to show us all that striving this complex thing called life doesn't mean that you're perfect, only that you're willing to show up for it every single bloody day. Bravo, Kevin!"

—**John M. Glionna**, Former Bureau Chief of *the Los Angeles Times*

"*The Art of Being Broken* takes us on a moving journey of struggle and strife to success, hope, and pure love of existence. Kevin Hines shares a vulnerable, harrowing, and powerful story of survival, triumph over adversity, and practical steps on how to survive pain and keep moving forward. It's a guide to readers on how to fight to always be here tomorrow because we need you here."

—**Justin Baldoni**, Producer, Writer, and Director and Founder of Wayfarer Studios

"Thirty years ago, no one was speaking publicly about surviving a suicide attempt. We only heard about the deaths. And, as a result, people struggling did so alone, fearing that literally no one else was experiencing the same heart-breaking pain as them. Kevin Hines's courage has been spreading and the impact is evident in the recovery journeys told in this book. It's the Papageno effect: healing, hope, and help get through and the power of sharing and caring is transformative!"

—**David W. Covington**, LPC, MBA, CEO and President of RI International

I've known Kevin Hines since he began sharing his story. The Glendon Association has brought Kevin to speak multiple times in and around Southern California. His presence is dynamic, and he is truly a walking miracle. His openness and psychological insight offer a valuable window into the suicidal process that we can all learn from. His new book, *The Art of Being Broken: How Storytelling Saves Lives*, is a moving piece of something so important... effective storytelling! Kevin's efforts have helped change lives all over the world. His journey and expertise is something to be shared with every person willing to do the work to better their brain and mental health! This book will positively alter the way you see the everything!

—**Dr. Lisa Firestone**, Clinical Psychologist, Author, and Director of Research and Education for The Glendon Association

"There is some science in Kevin Hines's *Art of Being Broken*, as it provides practical and effective instructions for building resilience for anyone facing serious mental health challenges. However, it is Kevin's artful telling of his personal story and the stories of his friends and colleagues that are most powerful, standing as testimonials to how we all can find gratitude through pain, hope through hopelessness, and meaningfulness through tragedy. It's gloriously ironic how a young man who sought to abandon life from a bridge emerged as a man who would forever build bridges...for those who would give up on themselves to those who will give all of themselves, with intention and purpose."

—**John Draper**, PhD, Founding Director of the National Suicide Prevention Lifeline

THE ART
OF
BEING
BROKEN

THE ART OF BEING BROKEN

HOW STORYTELLING SAVES LIVES

KEVIN HINES

Post Hill
PRESS

A POST HILL PRESS BOOK

The Art of Being Broken:
How Storytelling Saves Lives
© 2023 by Kevin Hines
All Rights Reserved

ISBN: 978-1-63758-852-9
ISBN (eBook): 978-1-63758-853-6

Cover design by Conroy Accord
Interior design and composition by Greg Johnson, Textbook Perfect

Although every effort has been made to ensure that the personal and professional advice present within this book is useful and appropriate, the author and publisher do not assume and hereby disclaim any liability to any person, business, or organization choosing to employ the guidance offered in this book.

This is a work of nonfiction. All people, locations, events, and situation are portrayed to the best of the author's memory.

No part of this book may be reproduced, stored in a retrieval system, or transmitted by any means without the written permission of the author and publisher.

Post Hill Press
New York • Nashville
posthillpress.com

Published in the United States of America
3 4 5 6 7 8 9 10

To my lovely wife, Margaret.
You are my greatest gift. You are my angel.
Our love is endless.
Thank God for you.

Contents

He is artistic yet pragmatic
He is quick witted yet well-tempered.
He walks, not runs, and lives well.
His words are filled with wisdom.
He is as timeless as the day is long.
He has two equal opposites.
He is up, he is down.
He is manic, he is depressed.
He understands the art of being broken.
He is the broken bipolar mind.

—KH

Foreword

By Zak Pym Williams

The first time I learned about Kevin's work was at a screening of his documentary *Suicide: The Ripple Effect* at San Francisco's Kabuki Theater. At that time, I had heard about his advocacy work, and his film was talked about positively among the other board members of the San Francisco Film Society, but it wasn't until I heard him speak in the film that I started to get an understanding of how inspirational and courageous a human being he truly was. That night, I left the screening inspired and hoping to meet him.

As fate would have it, I would meet Kevin in person a year later as we found ourselves speaking at the same event at the Mall of America in Minnesota for People Incorporated's fiftieth anniversary. During that event, I witnessed an incredible advocate get on stage and captivate the audience with his charisma and passion. Seeing him speak at that moment helped me understand what taking advocacy to a major-league level looked like. In entrancing me and the rest of the crowd with his energy, passion, and poise, Kevin convinced me that we all need to take every ounce of our strength and energy and apply it to making an impact.

After the event, I went for a walk with Kevin and his colleague in the empty Mall of America while he opened up about the anxiety and apprehension he experiences when traveling, and we started talking through our shared journey in dealing with our personal issues as we seek to help others heal and learn more about themselves. It was during his talk that Kevin helped me understand the profound strength and resilience that vulnerability brings. We've been friends ever since.

Since that evening, I've had the great privilege of spending many more hours with Kevin and his wonderful wife, Margaret, and am proud to call him a friend and thought partner in tackling taxing and trying issues relating to the parallel epidemic made up of the collective mental health crises of our communities. The more time we spend together, the more certain things become extremely apparent: Kevin is just getting started. There is so much more that needs to be done to make a lasting difference and he's showing up for every second of doing the work that needs to be done. Kevin is the definition of a true advocate. His authenticity, conviction, resilience, and unrelenting focus are what inspired me and so many others to take on supporting mental health as a life mission.

Kevin, on behalf of myself, my family, and the countless of people you've impacted, thank you for doing everything you do.

Preface

The Golden Gate Bridge, one of the most beautiful structures in the world and an iconic emblem of San Francisco, California. The bridge is also, sadly, a magnet to those determined to take their lives by suicide. Thankfully, the suicide deterrent net has been constructed and today prevents anyone from taking their lives at the GGB. How many have jumped? No one knows for sure, because not all jumps are witnessed, but the estimate is three thousand or higher.

How many have survived? I am one—one of only thirty-nine people who have survived the fall. I am one of just five who have regained full physical health and mobility. I am the sole survivor who dedicates his life's work to speaking openly about suicide awareness and learning the art of being broken. Living inside a broken mental and behavioral health system with a broken mind can be incredibly exhausting. You're always fighting to come out ahead. As I fight for mental well-being, I accept that I have been broken, both physically and mentally. And I know there is an art to being broken. There is a science to survival during unrelenting, lethal emotional pain. Thus, I have mastered the art of being broken.

And so can you.

I leapt off the bridge because I was told I must—told by the voices in my head, a symptom of my mental illness, bipolar disorder type I with psychotic features. This is the very same disease both of my biological parents were diagnosed with, only they called it manic depression in their day. It's a diagnosis I have lived with for over twenty-three years.

The purpose of my first book, *Cracked, Not Broken: Surviving & Thriving After a Suicide Attempt*, which came out in 2013, was to introduce the world to my story, my advocacy, and my mental health regimen and routine for wellness. *Cracked, Not Broken* was a bestseller for over six years and constantly sold out at book signings and events. From its release in 2013 until 2020, *Cracked, Not Broken* has proved a consistent seller and a book that resonates with audiences worldwide, who can't help but spread the word to others. While continuing and deepening my mission, *The Art of Being Broken: How Storytelling Saves Lives* is different from *Cracked, Not Broken* in so many ways. I have gleaned so much about how to reach people in mental pain who are living with suicidal ideation. I've learned that my thoughts—our thoughts—do not have to become our actions. Our thoughts do not have to own, rule, or define what we do next. They can simply be our thoughts, never leading us to attempt to die or die by our hands. I could not have anticipated after my attempt, and after my first book was published, that I would be living with chronic thoughts of suicide. Having now lived with them for two decades, I know exactly how to defeat them with resilience and gratitude. Gratitude and resilience are the two most protective factors from suicide. They are the two most powerful tools when fighting suicidal thoughts or ideas. Along my journey, I could not have anticipated that I'd be married now for over fifteen years and been together with my wife for eighteen. I have given over six thousand keynote speeches on my story in locations all around the world. More importantly, I would never have seen the birth of my two lovely godchildren, Zoey and Judah. I would never have seen my father become the best man at my wedding and there is so much more you will read about in this new book. Recovery is a constant. I am not recovered; no, I live in recovery daily just like one would from substance-use issues. It has proven to be quite the adventure. I am learning as much about the people my story has touched and affected as I am about myself.

The main takeaway is that pain is universal. I've traveled to all fifty states, and nearly every continent with my message of hope. I have spoken to those without hearing and those without sight. Each time I hear back from people on how my story has saved or changed their lives, it never ceases to amaze me that all of us have a role to play in suicide prevention, instilling hope, and helping people find the proverbial light at the end of the tunnel. *The Art of Being Broken* will retell the main aspects of my story for readers who aren't familiar; however, the retellings will be dramatically streamlined, revealing aspects of my journey that weren't covered in my first book. This new book will reveal the story of me being on the brink of death at the tipping point of Stevens-Johnson syndrome: my insides nearly boiled outside of me when one of my psychiatric medications poisoned my organs and caused nearly irreparable damage. For the better part of two years, it made me manic and as the doctors said, "It was akin to brain damage!" You'll read the story of how I fought that new skin disease and overcame it with the help and guidance of my lovely wife, Margaret. Then the story of Margaret's mother passing away in 2014 of lung cancer after smoking for over thirty years. Due to this incredible loss, Margaret could no longer be in our former favorite city, San Francisco. (Everything in that city reminded her of her mom/best friend.) We moved to Atlanta, Georgia, and I was awarded CNN's Champion of Change by Dr. Sanjay Gupta. Various online videos across all socials and multimedia platforms about my story have amassed well over two billion views. Hundreds of thousands of messages have come to me saying that my story saved, changed, or altered lives in a positive way forever. *The Art of Being Broken* is for newcomers and longtime supporters alike, providing a behind-the-scenes look at my story that hasn't appeared anywhere else. It will also chart the exciting new chapter of my life and a continued mission to help others #BeHereTomorrow and every single day after that.

The depiction of my subsequent relapses and ten hospitalizations in psychiatric lockdown units are raw, heartfelt, and honest. With this book, I'm sending a powerful message: Get help. Follow a science-based, evidence-informed treatment plan. Suicide is never the answer to any problem; it is the problem. Wellness can and will be achieved with hard work.

I am uniquely qualified to present this amazing story. Who else can speak with firsthand experience about the plunge from the Golden Gate Bridge? My life was cracked wide open, but now I understand there is an art to being broken, and a unique kind of healing that can come from triumph over such incredible adversity. Yet this is not just a typical triumph over adversity story. Instead, this book gives real-world examples of how people with severe brain pain can find hope, healing, and recovery; lose it all; and gain it back again.

My goal in all that I do is to bring hope to others living with brain diseases, mental health challenges, and brain pain as a professional storyteller, advocate, activist, and filmmaker who addresses audiences ranging from five hundred people to tens of thousands five to ten times a week. So far, I've told well over a million people in person and over a billion through social media campaigns, media interviews, books, documentaries, magazines, and viral online video for the largest short-form video media platforms that suicide is never the solution to any problem. My story was featured in the critically acclaimed film *The Bridge*, Eric Steel's 2006 documentary. Most recently, I've produced and directed a documentary, *Suicide: The Ripple Effect*, chronicling my life story that won nine international film awards including a BAFTA for Documentary of the Year! The film has been seen by over two million people in over twenty countries. More than five hundred people have said the film saved their lives.

Storytelling does save lives. Stories are twenty-two times more memorable than facts or statistics. There is great power in storytelling. There is an art and a science to storytelling and great storytellers can reach even the most broken of individuals. Stories don't simply lure us in, they scientifically affect the brains and minds of those who experience them. When I tell my story publicly, whether in person or through video media, those brains listening or viewing sync up with mine. The brain of the audience member is then showered with empathy and new neural pathways are even created, which can change the future behavior of said audience member. It is astonishing the positive impact the spoken and written word can have. I am ever so grateful I get the privilege to tell my story all around the globe.

The Art of Being Broken: How Storytelling Saves Lives has twenty-one chapters and over seventy thousand words. It is a beautiful account of a life well lived, filled with hope for the present and what is to come, no matter what pain is faced, and no matter what you are going through right now. Just because you are in a world of pain today doesn't mean you won't get to have a beautiful tomorrow, but you have to be here to get there in the first place.

Introduction

In the frigid, choppy waters below the Golden Gate Bridge in San Francisco, California, it was the sea lion I would affectionately name Herbert that came to my aid after my leap from said bridge to try and take my life. When the coast guard arrived at my position in the water, they were fully prepared to find my lifeless body under the GGB; they were shocked...I was alive, begging to be saved. After plucking me from the bay, they looked deep into my dark brown eyes and said,

"Do you know what you just did?!"

Fully conscious and aware, I replied, "Yes, I just jumped off of the Golden Gate Bridge!"

"Why?"

I said, "I don't know. I thought I had to die."

They responded with, "Do you know how many people we pull out of these waters that are already dead?"

My quick response was, "No, and I don't want to know."

Their retort, "Well, we're gonna tell ya anyway. This unit alone has pulled twenty-six dead bodies from these waters and only one live one...*you!*"

On that day, under a thin, harsh green blanket provided by those heroic coasties, I was strapped in a stretcher while a neck brace was put on me. I made a cognitive decision, a promise to myself. No matter the pain I would find myself in the future, I'd never again attempt to take my life. Suicide was and is no longer an option. My attempt occurred in the year 2000, twenty-three years ago.

Life has been filled with struggle and pain, but since my attempt I have learned that pain is inevitable. It's coming for all of us if it hasn't already, in some way, shape, or form, but suffering is optional. It's a choice. Happiness is also a choice, no matter the pain you are in. I have had hundreds of thousands of incredible experiences with people who say my story saved or changed their lives forever. These amazing people have reached out to me over the last two decades after my keynotes, events, and multimedia storytelling efforts to let me know how transformative they found my messages of hope.

These interactions have helped not only me in the wake of my jump but also countless others. They say that people who volunteer for a positive and productive cause are 63 percent more mentally healthy than those who do not. This is because giving and receiving respect from others releases chemicals in the brain that make people feel good, valued, and loved. It gives them purpose in more ways than one. It's truly scientific. I began my public speaking career volunteering for several suicide prevention and mental health organizations. Through them, I donated my time and keynotes for at least the first six years of speaking publicly. In doing so, I've learned quite clearly that helping others has helped me balance my overall well-being. The greatest part about this is that learning to hold gratitude in pain and gleaning how to be resilient in the face of it can all be taught *and shared*. I have had unbelievable adventures traveling around the world, sharing my story with millions of people who are searching for hope in their darkest hours. Following are several messages I have received over the years from individuals who heard my story on a viral video, saw me speak, read my book, or listened to me on a podcast. They sent me these various kind words. I receive them daily.

Hi Sir, I know that you probably get this a lot but you Mr. Kevin Hines saved my life. You truly and honestly saved me. Here's my story. Growing up everything was all over the place. In the beginning of my last year in elementary school, I started getting bullied bad. I'd go home, not talk to anyone in the house and I repeated that cycle for months until I self-harmed for the first time. It was scary and I didn't know what I was doing so I stopped. Then all throughout my middle school years I attempted to die by suicide seven different times in just three years of schooling. My dad was very disappointed in me and didn't understand. My mom was my light. She always believed I would get better because she went through it as well. I believed her for a little bit but then for some reason, I stopped believing in the person who believed in me. Now we come to where you saved my life.

I'm in 9th grade in high school and I am only 14 years old, but two weeks ago I tried to overdose because I was just so tired of fighting and living and I was confused. I didn't know how to feel or act. I grabbed every pill I could find. It didn't matter what it was, I just didn't care. I just didn't want to live. Once I took everything, I laid in my bed thinking about what I had just done. I didn't feel remorse. I didn't feel bad, I didn't feel anything. I just began scrolling on YouTube trying to find something to watch as time passed. Then while scrolling I see one of your videos telling your story and I thought about watching it, but I kept scrolling because I've seen it many other times. Then I stopped scrolling and I just had a feeling that I needed to watch your video. I scrolled back up and began watching. Not even a minute in and I just started sobbing, because I knew that this permanent solution was not going to fix all these temporary problems.

In the middle of watching and listening to your story I called my local police station. I told them my intentions, I told them what I took, and I told them I felt weak. The paramedics came and got me and on the way to the emergency room the paramedic looked at me and asked me why I wanted to do this and why I stopped myself. I told him my reasoning and I told him that

Introduction

I was watching a video of Kevin Hines telling his story and he looked at me again with an interesting glaze on his face. Then he told me that your story also saved his girlfriend. Sir, your story is so powerful and moving and I wish the whole world could know it. You saved not only my life but many many many others. You are amazing and I wish you well always."

—**Anonymous**

I don't know if you remember me...But we met in a Starbucks in Buckhead one afternoon a little over two years ago. I was the homeless guy who gave up after losing his 11-year-old daughter to a car crash. I lost all hope, lost my job, my home, everything...I was siting [sic] in Starbucks with all of my personal belongings (in a bag) and you were siting [sic] next to me. You looked at me and said "I like to talk to random people and just get to know them, get to know their story. Can I ask you a question? If you could change anything in your life, what would it be?" I told you my situation and what had happened to me, then you told me your story. We talked for almost an hour, and you bought me almost all the food in Starbucks I could possibly carry, gave me a bunch of wristbands and T-shirts to sell to put some money in my pocket and gave me your personal phone number. I thank you for just talking to me. I didn't know if I wanted to be on this earth anymore after what I'd went through. I want you to know that I got a job a week later, after months of work and sleeping outside in the dirt behind a Waffle House in Lindbergh Plaza, I rented my own apartment. I now am a manager at a car dealership, and I thank God and you for that chance encounter. Sincerely, The Stranger from Starbucks

—**@brOOtal_bananas**

I drove to a bridge near where I live. I was suicidal. The only thing that stopped my feet from leaving the ground were your words, your story about the day you jumped. About how you said that

the moment your feet left the ground you regretted it. That state-
ment kept me alive. Thank you, Kevin. I'm getting help now.

—@wendyaliseallen

You saved my life man!!! I tried to attempt a few weeks ago and
got very close. And every time I get back in that mind zone of
wanting to attempt, I listen to your story, and it helps me get out
of that!!

—@Saturnsstardust

When I was in middle school you came and talked to our school. I
saw an article about you retelling that story today. I just wanted
to let you know that I have kept your story with me and told it
to people for years. The part where you say "the moment my
hands left that rail instant regret" specifically rang in my head
and is something I pass on. I pride myself on being a positive, kind
person, and what you said to us in 7th grade influenced part of
who I am today. Thank you so much!

—@TheyCallMeCobaiinJayden

You're a good man just seen your story. Amazing a lighthouse on
the stormy sea's [sic] to so many people that are going through
the exact same thing you went through. With everything that's
going on in the world we need more people like you to help guide
humanity. You're a true inspiration and a beacon of hope.

—@Conrad_Reid44

I just want to say thank you and that I love you brother ♥ you
helped me reach help a year ago when I watched a video on you.
Thank you and I hope you are doing great. You possibly saved me
from doing the worst. Thank you!

—@aaaaj.r

Each one of these messages, notes, and letters move me to the core. I have never taken one of them for granted. They fuel my fire and passion to do this work daily. I am not alone in this endeavor to help save lives from suicide. There are thousands of young and older people alike, advocates sharing their stories of triumph over incredible adversity. There are heroes in the fields of mental, brain, mind, behavioral, spiritual, and physical well-being who are breaking down barriers and reaching people in their greatest moments of despair and helping them grow past their pain. Those leaders are baring their souls to change the lives and fates of others. These stories of pure hope have affected lives all over the galaxy in different ways. (Okay, maybe that's a stretch!) Or maybe not? One of those incredible advocates and a friend of mine, Makayla Nichols, sent some amazing stories to the moon. Literally out of this world. When I receive just one of these thank-you letters, I save them in a file, read each of them a few times, and share every single one with my wife, mom, dad, and a select few others. Then I sit down with my thoughts, quietly, alone, and take stock in what it means to care for others. After that, I pray to God to give me the strength to continue sharing my story because as much as I am passionate about it, it is hard to do.

Some of the greatest experiences I have are people coming up to me at public events and saying something to the effect of "because of the words you just spoke, I am no longer going to take my life." Years ago, when I began speaking for the United States military, I spoke to over ten thousand marines at Camp Lejeune over two days. There, the most incredible thing happened. After my second day of keynote addresses, so many marines walked up to me to shake my hand after an uproarious standing ovation. Then one young man, a lance corporal, maybe four or five years into his time in the armed forces, stood in front of me and said, "Ya know, I wasn't going to come to your stupid speech. I thought it was just going to be another useless death by PowerPoint piece of bull$%*!

But I decided to attend, and I am glad I did." As he spoke, he began removing his lance corporal chevron, or rank pin. "I was going to kill myself today. Now I am going to ask for help. Would you mind walking me to my CO [commanding officer]?" Right after saying that, he placed his rank pin on my beige sport coat lapel. We then walked together to his CO. This kind of reaction happens every day. For more than the last two decades, it has emboldened me to continue the work. It's what *I* do it for.

Changing destinies, fates, and futures is powerful stuff. I don't own what happens here. I've never saved a life. I say words, people hear those words, they go home, or sit with their thoughts. They do the work; they save and change their own lives. It's the same for brain health advocates around the globe. Simply put, we are only conduits, cogs in the wheel of time, using the gift of gab to help alter lives forever. We, the collective who have conquered our pain, share how we #CNQRPAIN in every corner of the world. People hear our messages of light, self-love, and hope, then they find it within themselves to hustle hard for their mental well-being. There is an art to being well, and moreover, there is an art to being broken. We share both arts with every nation with the wish and prayer that it hits home in the hearts of those living in complete darkness, destitution, and despair.

There is great value in storytelling. In fact, it has been a part of every known culture since the dawn of mankind. From the ancient Egyptian hieroglyphics to the drawings of cavemen, to the Old West's traveling storytellers. Stories, whether written or spoken, have altered the course of history since their inception. Take the Bible, for instance—arguably the greatest, most widely read, and retold story in existence. It has been translated to every known language, heard, and retold to congregations everywhere and across every continent. I think about this level of connection we have to each other all the time. I think about the hundreds of thousands of messages I've acquired over the twenty plus years doing this. Then

I think about the people who say I saved their lives. Then I think about how that ripple effect changed the course of their parents', siblings', loved ones', and significant others' lives. My only sadness is that I cannot reach everyone. For every twenty letters I receive thanking me, I get one letter from someone so determined to die by suicide that they say nothing I do or say can change their minds. Because I am only one man, I cannot possibly reach back to every-one who seeks me out. It breaks my heart. I am no world savior; I have no God complex. Ultimately, I am a simple human who loves life, appreciates every waking moment, is grateful for every place I get to go, and more importantly, is humbly appreciative to every person who reads or hear my words. I live in the present. Never have I claimed to be anything else.

In my daily struggle with bipolar depression, the very same brain disease both my biological parents had before me, I break down on the regular; the struggle is oh so real. I think about my destitute biological parents who died from drugs and alcohol, who truly died tragically from their lack of mental wellness and brain well-being. They never got to tell their incredible stories. But it is what I know of their short lives that keeps and has always kept me away from drugs. I binge drank in high school and until I was twenty-one years old (I haven't had a sip since then). When I think of drinking or getting drunk, my mother's and father's stories come to mind; they stop me every time. I tell stories for a living; I tell stories because I know it helps save and change lives. I tell stories because it is how we grow and change culture, society, and the world.

When you read *The Art of Being Broken*, the much-anticipated, better-late-than-never sequel to *Cracked, Not Broken*, try to hear my voice in your head. Try to find the needed light at the end of your tunnel. And if you picked it up because you are in immeasurable pain, know that I am with you. We are with you. You can and will conquer your pain. I got you. *The Art of Being Broken* is the essential next chapter to my story, a story that has been credited with saving so many lives. I still receive letters, social media posts, and comments from all over the world from people who have read the book and found their lives changed.

Chronicling these next chapters in my life through this new book will share so much more of my journey. I see success of this book not in monetary gain, but in the lives changed from reading it. The lives completely transformed by soaking these stories of hope in. I foresee this book *The Art of Being Broken* or TaoBB translated into multiple languages and reaching a much, much larger audience. This new book includes the story of how I met and fell in love with my adoring wife and best friend, Margaret Hines. This new book will cover my twenty-six electroshock therapy treatments, which changed me forever. It covers my remaining psychiatric ward stays and my near-death experience having been on the tipping point of the skin disease, Stevens-Johnsons Syndrome. It's going to be an epic true tale of hope, redemption, and recovery that if published globally will alter the lives of millions. The goal is to help as many human beings as possible #BeHereTomorrow and every single day after that. This is my life's mission, my journey; this is our journey. Walk this path with me. Read the rest of this book, let it into your heart, and heed the lessons learned along the way. Always be true to yourself, who you are at your core. Know I care about you, know you are loved, and know you matter. You are meant to be here until your natural end. You, my friends reading my book, are gifts to me, not the other way around.

THE ART
OF
BEING
BROKEN

CHAPTER 1

The Day of My Attempt

The room smelled of old socks, and all I could hear was the ticktock of the sharply echoing white-rimmed clock on the wall above my uncomfortable hospital bed. I laid there immobile after my attempt. Jumping from the Golden Gate Bridge would prove to be the greatest mistake I would ever make. Surviving said jump would alter the course of my life forever. Unable to move, I became in tune with the sounds of the ward. Footsteps constantly shuffling up and down the hallways. Doctors, nurses, and staff voices humming in the background. Then it became clear, a familiar footfall: my father was striding quickly to reach my room, the click of his familiar footfalls. Immediately, I knew Patrick Kevin Hines, my namesake, and his work loafers were closing in. The footsteps became louder; he grew closer. Then they stopped right at my door.

His voice was shaky. "Kevin, I'm sorry!"

My reply was faint, nearly inaudible, and full of so much pain, "No, Dad, I'm sorry." He took a position at the foot of my bed, looked at me, and for the first time in all my nineteen years, I witnessed my father crying. I didn't know the man had tear ducts. I watched helplessly as waterfalls fell from his eyes.

"Kevin, you are going to be okay. I promise!" As he came to my left side, his body leaned in, and he kissed my forehead gently. My caring father would not leave my side for four and a half weeks. No shower, no shave, he simply washed up in my tiny hospital bathroom daily. Each night as I slept, he sat by my side, grasping my hand, and praying intensely to the Lord above that I would survive, let alone be able to walk. Living with me for the last few years had not been easy for him. We fought constantly, arguing and engaging in yelling matches that should have had the police called for domestic disturbance.

Bipolar depression had taken its hold on me for the two years prior to my attempt. Its symptoms were the reason I was kicked out of my mother's house on my eighteenth birthday. I empathized with her decision. Living with my dad, we both raged like rival barking dogs.

All Pat Hines could think as I laid helpless in that bright, white hospital room, bedpan under me, and a catheter painfully placed inside me, was: "What if my oldest son dies?" Nearly twenty years post jump, I asked my father if he still fears my death by suicide. His answer? "Kevin, every time the phone rings." He did not mean when I call him; he meant every time his cell phone goes off in his pocket, his first and every thought is *Is Kevin alive?* Once he told me, "Kevin, if you had died that day, I would have died."

On the day of my attempt, September 25 of the year 2000, all those years ago, Debi Hines sat quietly in a CEU class learning about loved ones with depression and bipolar disorder. The very day she received the call that I had just attempted to resign from this world by leaping off the most popular suicide spot in the known universe. Much like my father, she too embarked on a fear and tear-filled journey to Marin General Hospital. She was actually the very first to arrive. Unbeknownst to me, the week before I jumped off the bridge, my mom's work had given their employees pagers. To her, it felt like an electronic leash. She held her work off for a week saying she didn't want to wear the pager. Finally, she took the pager and wore it after her boss insisted. The morning of my attempt she entered the class previously mentioned for her continuing education units. The class was called "Understanding Depression." It was being held in Oakland, California. She told Libby, my sister, that she would be in Oakland for this class. She left Libby her pager number. At 10:15 a.m., my mom called her friend, Butch, and said, "They should have just put Kevin's picture on the screen." In the class, she learned of traumatic brain damage done to a set of monkeys who had all been part of a study of the brain's reaction to the removal from their mothers at birth. When I was an infant, I was removed from my birth mother five times. I was even kidnapped from foster care by my birth parents. Then they returned me to foster care when they could no longer care for me and my brother, Jordache. Then he and I got bronchitis, and he died.… The closest person to me. The doctor would eventually do a literal million-dollar workup on me after I landed in the Hines home—rather, after they planned to make me their son. He determined after test after test that I had bowel irritability secondary to emotional trauma, a full-blown attachment disorder, and severe abandonment issues. These would follow me the reminder of my life. I still deal with them today.

Back to the day of my attempt. At 10:30 a.m., my mom hung up with her friend, Butch. She walked into the classroom and her pager went off. Libby called; my mom almost wasn't gonna pick up the phone to call her back. When she did call Libby, my sister said, "Mom, the coast guard picked up Kevin this morning; he jumped off the Golden Gate Bridge. He's still alive."

My mom, as a nurse who would rack up a total of fifty years spending time working in the neuro ward, asked, "Is he breathing on his own?"

Lib said, "I don't know."

My dear mom said, "Stay by the phone and I will call you back." My mom turned around near a table with several women and she said aloud and befuddled, "I have to leave; my son just jumped off of the Golden Gate Bridge."

The woman at the table said, "What's your name?"

She said, "Debi Hines."

The woman gave her eight hours of credit toward her CEUs, which she hadn't even earned.

My mom then called her friend again and said, "I need to know specific directions from Hagenburger Road in Oakland." She got in her car to get to the freeway, her friend, Butch gave her specific directions since it was the year 2000 and GPS was near nonexistent. She thanked him, hung up, and called her mom, Gramma Kay, and that's when she started to cry.

Gramma Kay said, "I'll go over to Libby, and I will pick up Joseph."

My mom cried profusely and prayed to God, "God, please let him stay alive so I can kiss him, but if he's gonna be like Christopher Reeve, please let me kiss him, then take him." She thought, *Who hears about someone surviving a jump off the Golden Gate Bridge?*

She arrived at the hospital and the chaplain approached her; she wasn't receptive. The doctor approached her.

She asked, "Is he breathing on his own?"

He said, "He's breathing on his own and wiggling his toes. He's moving his hands and legs and is wide awake."

My mom was blown away. "WHAT?!"

The doctor said, "He's up getting a CT scan now and they'll bring him up from radiology to the ICU." Mom went to the ICU, and my father, Patrick, entered the hospital wing with his secretary. He said, "I couldn't drive and needed her to drive me because I was so upset." I was then wheeled into my hospital room where my mom counted to three alongside the transport orderly, two nurses, and a doctor. They then moved me from the gurney to the ICU hospital bed. My mom said, "Hi, Kevin."

I looked at her and said, "Mom, it was hecka dark and hecka cold."

"Kevin, God must have wanted you here for a reason. I guess he wanted you to win that Oscar."

I had done high school and eventually college theater and taken a few acting in front of the camera classes. A week prior to my attempt, I went to my mom's house to say hi and tell her how well I was doing. I neglected to tell her my then girlfriend had broken up with me. On the day of my suicide attempt, I was emotionally and physically tired. After my parents' initial visit to the hospital, it was just a waiting game to see the extent of my injuries. My mom left for her home and called her best friend Janet, Janet's mom, Gramma Kay, and several others to let them know my health status. The worst part for her was having to cross the Golden Gate Bridge in her car—coming down the hill approaching the bridge, crossing it, feeling completely surreal in the moment. She got home, and Libby, Joseph, and Gramma Kay could not believe it.

Mom then called into work at the mental health clinic where she was a nurse. She said to herself, *How did I fail him? I work in the field, what signs did I miss?* She then came every day to see me. The very next day, there was an office directly off the nurse's station where I was resting. The discharge manager wanted to talk to my mom and dad, trying to find out my insurance coverage. My mom said to her, "Kevin was a foster child and had medical insurance until three weeks ago. He should be able to get his medical reinstated."

Pat said, "I'm taking care of this; you don't have to answer any of these questions." He put his insurance down.

Day one, I jumped. Day two, they took a closer look at my injuries. Day three, I underwent a ten-and-a-half-hour surgery for my back. They replaced three shattered vertebrae with titanium and added four pins, one cylindrical metal cage, and a titanium plate to my left side, which is the singular reason I get the privilege to stand, walk, and run. I was discharged in just weeks and was wearing a back brace and walking with a cane at my first psychiatric ward. My mom, Gramma Kay, and my little brother Joseph came to visit me. I invited them into my room to meet my roommates. I was unbeliev-ably manic. I said, "They're the best roommates in the world." When they left, Gramma Kay said, "God, it feels like we just sent him off to college and he was showing off his dorm room."

I even said to them, "Can I offer you something to eat or some-thing to drink?"

My mom would look at my life in hindsight and say I was so much more sensitive than most kids, and everything that happened to or around me was so dramatic. She doesn't know if she'd call my behavior as a child manic, but I was certainly more easily affected by the people and things around me. I was easily hurt and often devastated by certain situations that might not affect others in the same way. I was on Tegretol from age ten to age sixteen after a grand mal epileptic seizure. By the age of sixteen, I'd had no seizures for so long they took me off my epilepsy medications. They did not know at the time that the meds they had me on were also mood stabilizers and hindering my bipolar disorder from rearing its ugly head. My mood stabilization went away, and my mood was rocked. My then doctor believed I had a catastrophic response to my parents' divorce, which had occurred prior to my attempt, right after I had been taken off Tegretol.

My big sister and little brother were devastated. Everybody was.

For the first few weeks in the physical ward prior to entering the psych ward, I was a bubble boy; very few people were allowed to come in and out of my room. Aside from the doctors, nurses, and staff, it was only my immediate family that could visit. Mom showed up every single day. Dad lived there by my side. What a blessing to have so much care, compassion, and love. I've never taken it for granted. The day I jumped, I couldn't see straight. Illogical and irrational thoughts rang true in my mind. Prior to my attempt, the auditory hallucinations had overwhelmed my soul. *You have to die. You are useless, Kevin. Everyone hates you. Your family will be better off without you!* The torment was palpable...seemingly inescapable.

Very soon after my arrival at the hospital, the letters, cards, and notes began to flood in. Letters from people I had not heard from in five to seven years. Well wishes and blessing cards came in by the dozens. Prayers were said and masses were held across the city of San Francisco. My high school filled a massive strip of sheet paper with signatures and notes to get well soon. All my friends asked, "Why didn't you call me?"

The day it occurred—the day I nearly lost my destiny by my hands—the bridge was its usual overcrowded hotspot. There were bikers, awe-inspired tourists, panting joggers, dedicated runners, and hyperaware police officers out looking for threats or issues of any kind. They were searching for suicidal individuals and two officers passed me by more than once that day. In all fairness, those officers had not been trained in suicide prevention. Today they are, and today they save between 50 to 120 lives a year, which is incredible. Today they have a plan and protocol for these situations. Back then, however, they had no protocol for me. The forest-green water beneath the bridge was choppy, rough, apparently six currents move simultaneously and sometimes violently in different directions under that bridge. Wind levels were high on September 25, 2000. Opaque gray and pasty white fog ruled the air. It was a typical overcast day in the city by the bay. Tired...I was so tired of the voices in my head, so tired of the battle I'd been waging for the better part of two years. The denial of my brain illness ran from my head down through my gut. All I needed that day was to ask for help. My dear ol' dad tried to stay with me that day. He knew I was unwell, but he was not trained in suicide prevention techniques; what parent is before it's too late? Fooling my father was easy. Pretending to be okay had become second nature to me. I had gotten great at something a large number of people are really, really great at these days: silencing my pain. If you, reading this now, are going to learn one thing from me, learn this: don't learn the hard way like I did, and never again silence your pain. I don't care if you are the toughest person you know. Unburden yourself, and unsilence your brain pain. Your voice deserves to be heard; your voice matters; your pain is worthy of my time and that of others. Suicide never has to be the solution to your problems because it *is* the problem. You are valued, loved, worthy, important, and you matter to me. Back to that day...

The moment my shaky hands left the rail, instantaneous regret filled my disjointed mind.

One—I was falling headfirst to the waters below the bridge.

Two—If I hit headfirst, I would surely die. I prayed, "What have I just done! I don't want to die, God, please save me!"

Three—I was rotating my head back, turning my body in midair by sheer will, flying downward between seventy-five to eighty miles an hour, and closing in on terminal velocity.

Four—Impact and implosion. Fifteen thousand pounds of pressure usually results in catastrophic destruction to the human body. There are tens of ways to die off the Golden Gate Bridge according to my good friend and the former Marin Coroner, Ken Holmes, and they're mostly slow and violent!

Four seconds is all it takes to erase a life off the famed and storied GGB.

Five—A vacuum sucked my shattered body seventy feet beneath the surface!

Six—I opened my eyes. I was alive, and I was drowning. Freaking out and frantic, I swam in any direction. I didn't know which way was up or down.

Seven, eight, nine, ten—I could not feel my legs although they were working. I was going further down; the water got murkier, darker, greener, grotesque.

Eleven, twelve, thirteen—My ears began to ring. My eyes began to bulge. The pressure was immense. Recognizing my mistake, I shot for what I believed to be the surface, moving as fast as my arms would take me. I went seventy feet in one breath. One goal...*to live!*

While my body broke through the surface, my mind raced. The water was freezing! I could not die here. I prayed, "God, please save me; I made a mistake. God; please save me; I don't want to die! I made a mistake!" Those six fluctuating and unpredictable currents kept me from being able to swim to the rocks at Fort Baker. Unbeknownst to me, so many things were in play. People above the bridge who witnessed my leap from it called the bridge patrol, and a flare was sent down near my position in the water for the coast guard, which was en route. A woman driving by saw me go over the rail and called a friend in the coast guard. The reason they reached me in a timely manner before my body would set into hypothermia and drown was because of this woman's bold and immediate action and phone call. Prior to the coasties' arrival, something very large, very slimy, and very, very alive began circling beneath me. I thought, *Of course, I didn't die jumping off of the Golden Gate Bridge, so now a shark is going to eat me!* Terrified, I awaited a huge shark bite–sized chunk to be taken from any, or all, of my extremities.

It didn't. Eventually, my fear and torment turned to wonderment and pure curiosity. This creature beneath me was circling faster and faster. No longer was I treading or wading in the water. I laid above the water on my back, being bumped to the surface regularly by this mammal. Sometime later, I learned it was, in fact, a sea lion. Right then and there, on that day, I named him, Herbert. Herbert was the first of many to save my life that day. Thank you, Herbert, wherever you are! More on Herbert later!

The coast guard officers were astounded to see that this was a true rescue, not just another dead body recovery. These fine souls were the second to save my life that day. They told me right there on their flat board on the boat when they grabbed me from the icy waters, "Do you know what you just did?"

"Yeah, I was there," I replied.

The most senior officer leaned in. "Do you know how many people we pull from these waters that are already dead?"

"No, and I don't want to know."

"Well kid, were gonna tell ya anyway. This unit alone, this year alone, has pulled twenty-six dead bodies from these waters, and only one live one. You!" A harsh green blanket was put over me. I had a neck brace on and was strapped into the flat board. I wasn't going anywhere even if I wanted to. This was nothing short of a miracle. Although, I do have a friend who is fond of saying that it was purely binary. All ones and zeros. That by sheer probability, it had to happen to someone the way it happened to me.

However, that friend lacks faith, faith that I have in droves. It would be faith, family, and friends (and a whole lot of therapy) that would get me through the next twenty-one years living with chronic physical pain and chronic thoughts of ending my life. Just as I was grasping what I had done, the boat posted up at the dock nearest the coast guard station, an awaiting ambulance in tow.

My breathing was erratic; my heart was palpitating. It felt like I was having a heart attack. My exercise-induced asthma was out of control. My inhaler was in my left pocket, but the EMTs could not allow me to take an inhalation just in case I had ruptured my lungs or had any other kind of serious internal injuries prohibiting me from using my inhaler due to potential detriment to my over-all health and any chance of survival on the way to Marin General Hospital. Family would arrive very soon after I did, and they sent me into surgery three days into my stay, and thankfully, I survived. I even went on to thrive.

I want to stop here for a moment for those of you reading in lethal emotional pain right as you read this page. Please, once again, do not learn the hard way like I did. No matter your pain, suicide is not the solution. Trust me as someone who has survived these intrusive thoughts on countless occasions. I have gleaned how to value every waking moment of this life, even finding gratitude in the face of pain so I can be resilient from it.

A year to the date after my attempt, at the same time of my attempt, my father, Patrick, called me on my cell. He said, "Kev, I'm comin' to pick you up; we're going for a drive!"

I replied, "Great, where are we going, Dad?"

His response: "Like I said, for a drive!" Forty-five minutes later, he pulled up to the very same spot he dropped me off the day I tried to take my life a year prior. Right there at City College. I got in the car. The ride was silent; neither of us spoke. He drove and drove. We pulled onto 19th Avenue, then Park Presidio. He stopped on Clement St. and Park Presidio; I knew exactly where we were headed. He asked me to hop out of the car near what used to be the police officers' events building; police cars and bikes lined the parking lot. My dad asked me to pick a purple tulip with gold pollen inside from the building's garden. Top brass were in the windows, dressed in their blues for a law enforcement function. I was reluctant to pick a flower in SF as you are liable to get a fine. My dad yelled out the car, "Pick a gawd damn flower!" and when Pat Hines asks something of you twice, you do it.

We sped off and on our way to the GGB. I felt nauseous just thinking of going back to the bridge. Dad pulled into the parking lot. He looked at me, his eyes reaching into my soul. "Kevin, we have to do this. We need closure!"

I thought to myself, *You need closure, old man! I need to go home and lay down!* Something I'd never in my wildest imagination say out loud to my father. Stepping out of the car felt like a foreign experience. Still nauseous, growing more reluctant as we moved toward the walkway of that damn harbinger of death, we moved forward.

"Kevin, show me exactly where it happened. Show me the exact light rail."

I remember like it was yesterday. We slowly approached the very light rail where one year to the date we had nearly lost it all. My dad grabbed my left hand in his right, we said an Our Father and a Hail Mary, and he said "Drop the flower."

I did. It wafted down quite slowly, hit the water ever so gently, and immediately caused the tiniest of ripple effects (hence the name of the first documentary film I directed and produced, *Suicide: The Ripple Effect*) then, two feet to the right popped up a sea lion. This was arguably the most beautiful moment I have ever spent with my father, next to him being the best man at my wedding. There was no other choice. All my friends were pissed off.

CHAPTER 2

The Injuries

A young man was wheeled into the hospital the day after me. He, too, survived a jump from the Golden Gate Bridge. The doctors and nurses feared that it was my best friend at the time and politely requested that I be rolled into his room to see if he was indeed someone I knew. Thankfully, it was no one I was familiar with. I never learned if the young man survived. Ninety-nine percent of those who have leapt off that bridge never again get to tell their stories. Every one of them is gone forever. Their families mourn their loss each waking moment of every single day. I broke my family and friends' hearts with what I did.

Physically, I was broken. Three shattered vertebrae, a sprained ankle, and an unwavering, immeasurable, enormous amount of pain—physical, emotional, and mental. Eventually the morphine kept the physical pain at bay but caused powerful, daunting, and horrifying hallucinations. I saw things you wouldn't want to see in your worst nightmares. My initial memory of those who visited the hospital the first few days is shaky, although family and friends would recount it for me many times over. Even so, I never forgot my mother's, father's, sister's, and brother's first words when they saw me immobile, laid up, and the closest to death I'd ever been. I never forgot what it cost us.

Years later, when I asked my father on camera for my documentary film *Suicide: The Ripple Effect* if he still fears my death by suicide, his answer after telling me to "Turn off the camera! Kevin... Every time the phone rings." He didn't say when I call him, he said every time the phone goes off in his pocket, his first and every thought for the last two decades has been *Is Kevin alive?!* One of the biggest issues both my parents had to deal with was the fact that very few people asked them how they were feeling after what I did. People were so über focused on my recovery that very few folks outside of my immediate and extended family inquired as to how my little brother, older sister, Mom, and Dad were doing. They were not empathetic toward Debi and Pat Hines. One of my biggest regrets was that for years, even I did not adequately ask them how they were doing from what I had done on September 25, 2000. Even today, I haven't done an efficient job of holding space for them to unload and tell me their truths. I wish I worked harder to help them move forward. Today, I try and put myself in their shoes. I often think what they went through the moment they learned of my severe attempt. I am trying to improve the lines of communication with all my family and friends, to be there for any residual pain for what I did may still be causing.

This was my initiation heading into *The Art of Being Broken*. This was the beginning of a journey into the depths of mental illness, physical inability, and what was a shattered family trying to pick up the pieces. The injuries I sustained during my attempt and my subsequent survival allowed me the insight to see the world from a different point of view. After my surgery, I ended up briefly in a back brace and a wheelchair; for the time being, it was my only mode of transport. I could barely get around. In less than a week, I went from a wheelchair to a walker and a back brace, and from that walker to a back brace and a cane. It was a challenge to say the least, but in that challenge, I found hope. Over the last twenty-two years traveling and sharing my story, I have met tons of people who wished they hadn't survived their attempts, people who by all accounts still feel the desire to take their lives. For every ten people who've shared that darkness with me, I have met hundreds of thousands of people who have said they are so glad to be alive from their attempts.

When I was in that wheelchair, ever so briefly, I couldn't have felt more grateful in my life. It was ridiculously painful, but I was grateful despite such pain. Going from the wheelchair to poppin' wheelies in the hospital hallways, to wearing a back brace and walking super slowly with a walker took some getting used to. I felt the endurance of an eighty-nine-year-old grandfather of three. I moved at the pace of a dying snail. Even so, I was just so damn appreciative for my coveted second chance at life.

We can easily look at major life setbacks, struggles, hardships, or breakdowns as the final straw. If we lack gratitude for such pain, we cannot overcome it. Lacking gratitude for all life throws at you allows whatever trauma you experienced or will experience to own you. If you take back that control, that ownership, after such a traumatic incident(s) or event(s), and at the same time recognize that pain cannot, and should not define you, you will always win at the game of life. If you instead allow any such pain to own you, you will remain miserable forever. I had a choice: allow my attempt and my diagnosis to continue destroying me, or I could fight tooth and nail in an uphill battle against all my self-loathing, all my self-hate, and my inner critical voice. That way, no matter what happens to me, I defeat the greatest enemy of all (thanks, Joe Williams for this next bit): the enemy within!

You see, my friends, pain is universal. Pain is inevitable, but suffering is optional. It's a choice. Every clinician I used to have told me I was suffering. They said I was suffering from mental illness. They said I was suffering from depression. They said I was suffering from bipolar disorder. They said I was suffering from an eating disorder when I was, and I was. I then adopted this narrative that was handed to me on a silver platter and became a "sufferer." I wrote about suffering, spoke about suffering, even vlogged about suffering. That only made me the victim of my own story. It wasn't until I realized that I could fight my pain, battle my pain, live with my pain, and thrive despite of my pain that I realized I've been in pain since the day I was born and raised in a crack motel; but I've never suffered a day in my life, instead, I've been given a second chance at it. It's incredible: no matter the physical, emotional, or mental pain we are in, if we can find a way to hold gratitude in our pain, we can always be resilient, thus we can survive it. I'm not writing about those who've been the victims of serious abuse, raised in catastrophic environments, or victims of violent crimes (although I believe with help you can all recover too). I am writing specifically about those of us who struggle daily inside our fractured and broken minds from what "they" tell us is mental illness. We wonder why there is such a stigma (discrimination) against us. The word "mental" has a negative connotation all by itself. How many of you reading this want to be labeled or called mental? None of you do. I call it #brainpain. I'm talking about the teenager with depression and anxiety who gets bullied relentlessly and then turns to self-harm, then suicidal ideation, and maybe even attempts to take their life.

We have forgotten to teach our children the art and science of resilience. We are a nation of parents on mobile devices raising children on mobile devices. Instead of the hard work to teach our younger generations the power of using their voices to express themselves in appropriate and civilized ways, we are allowing them to search online for the answers to all their problems. We are allowing young minds that have not fully been developed to view things on social media, and through various means of entertainment that are completely inappropriate for their age. Minds are literally being corrupted and warped by things they are scientifically not ready to see.

The injuries our youth are experiencing to their brain's stability are heartbreaking. The injuries furthered by Covid's incredible cost and loss to the world's population has created a massive fallout of depression, panic, and severe brain pain. Covid-19 has triggered a 25 percent increase in depression and anxiety worldwide. My personal injuries after my attempt run parallel with the pain the globe is living through; they just exist on a much smaller scale. Instead, my world is affected by my bipolar diagnosis and near death. My mother, Debi, while I was in the hospital, would help me walk around the hospital unit with my walker and back brace. She would stay right by my side with the nurses to make sure my recovery journey was a safe one. Obviously, she's an incredible nurse herself. My father, Patrick, after my release from the psych ward took time off work to walk me from my bedroom to the bathroom because I could not shower by myself for fear of falling and reinjuring myself. My dad was for some time glued to my side, making sure at any moment I did not fall. All in all, I was so blessed to recover from my injuries; ultimately, they were mild compared to most who do what I did. My new level of gratitude knows no bounds. It took months to get out of the back brace and away from using the cane. I certainly had to hobble around for a bit with that brown cane. The day I lost it and could walk on my own with just my back brace was a massive accomplishment. I was thrilled. Slowly, I kept with my physical therapy daily, it was downtown in the same building of my future psychopharmacologist, Dr. Karin Hastik. She'd eventually save my life a couple of times some years later. I'm getting ahead of myself. Physical therapy was no joke. It was hard, emotional. I had to pace myself. I had setbacks but remained optimistic and it paid off.

I must thank my mom for my optimism; she carries hers in droves. Her glass is never half full or half empty—it's toppling over with optimism. We've had our problems but have a wonderful relationship today. As my mobility increased so did my confidence, and my brain health improved. Hard work was the key. The fact is not everyone has the kind of tremendous support network that I have. Knowing that, I ask you readers who are well, sane, and put together to reach out to your strong friends, those who seem fine. Those who could potentially be silencing their pain. We cannot simply wait for suicidal people or people in crisis or those struggling with brain pain to speak up and speak often. We who are well must reach out daily. These topics, mental health, and suicide prevention, must be brought up regularly at the breakfast, lunch, and dinner table.

The crisis text line has determined that by asking three important invaluable questions to someone who is potentially suicidal you can effectively save lives. "Are you thinking of killing yourself? Have you made plans to take your life? Do you have the means?" Asking, "Are you thinking of killing yourself?" gets a more honest answer than even the question "Are you thinking of suicide?" because of the taboo on the word suicide. It gets a more honest answer than "Are you self-harming?" because self-harm is not suicide—it's self-harm. You can text CNQR to 741741, the crisis text line, and by doing so when in crisis, we can track our active rescues. We can see when lives are saved, and so many have been. You can also call 988, the lifeline, to hear the voice of someone who cares; either way, trained crisis counselors will have your back and do their darndest to keep you safe, even from yourself.

I wish I knew about these resources before my attempt. I wish I had the numbers saved in my phone (parents, hint hint)! The injuries I recovered from but off and on, my brain was still broken. It wasn't easy after my attempt off the GGB. I live in recovery daily. One day at a time, one step at a time, and they're all baby steps. Sometimes, with my chronic back pain and the ease with which I throw out my back picking up a sock or getting in and out of bed, they are literally still baby steps. Sometimes, I still must pull my new black cane out and use it. Mentally, my injuries have persisted. The ups and downs of bipolar disorder can be unrelenting. Emotional disturbances occur, I cope, pivot, work very hard to correct, and move forward. I look to the living, thank God for this existence, and move forward in the face of inescapable pain. You can too! Don't let your pain defeat you; instead, let it build you brick by brick by brick from the ground up!

CHAPTER 3

The Gift of
Survival = Perspective

The day I leapt from the Golden Gate Bridge would change my life forever. It would lead me down a path of peril, pain, brokenness, despair, and an eternal struggle with finding a way to love myself entirely. I would live twenty-two years afterward often wondering why I got to survive. Yet one thing it did give me was perspective. When I was plucked from those waters by the coast guard, I made a cognitive decision that no matter the pain I'd be in again, I would never attempt to die by my hands. I made the decision to commit to life until I die of natural causes or lightning strikes me down wherever I stand. Today I take nothing for granted. I see my journey clearly. No matter the suicidal ideation that creeps in, and it does, I will not attempt. Instead, I will speak about it to anyone willing to listen. Anyone willing to hear my words, my brain pain. I will say, "I need help now!" It's not always the first, second, third, or even fourth person you turn to that will be able to handle such pain. Yet by the sheer probability and number of people you ask, surely someone will be able to empathize with your pain and help keep you safe. For over two decades, someone has always answered the call. Be bold, and demand the help you deserve. Do not accept suicidal ideations as your answer; they are the greatest liars we know.

The perspective I gained from my survival was unparalleled. When I laid immobile directly after my attempt inside the flat board of the coast guard boat, things came into crystal clear view. The officers who saved me from the waters beneath the bridge gazed upon my conscious body in disbelief. They were mesmerized at the fact that I had survived and was swimming in the waters before they picked me up.

They had already put my neck in a neck brace, strapped me in from head to toe, and cut off my upper-body clothing searching for hemorrhaging or internal bleeding signs. The most senior officer then said, "We have pulled twenty-six dead bodies from these waters this year alone, and only one live one…you!" I can tell you this gave me the greatest point of perspective I have ever received. Maybe will ever receive. On that day, I made a cognitive decision; no matter the suicidal ideations I may ever have in the future, I would never attempt to take my life again. If someone ever tells you Kevin Hines died by suicide, do me a solid: open an all-out investigation because it was a murder.

People say there is a stigma against those with mental illness. I say stigma is not the right word. It is intensely lacking. We don't call prejudice, bigotry, and hatred stigma; we call it prejudice, bigotry, and hatred. What is happening to those struggling daily with mental illness is purely discrimination based on something completely out of their control. Mental illness and addictions are two of the last diseases we still blame people for. Would you tell someone with liver, heart, lung, or kidney disease to "Snap out of it!", "Get over it!", "Move on!", "Pull yourself up by your bootstraps!", or "It's all in your head!?" No way! You'd show up at the hospital with a teddy bear, flowers, empathy, compassion, lack of any judgement, and care. You would do everything in your power to make the person feel better, and you'd do anything to help them find hope, healing, and recovery. Why can't we do the same thing for brain health? The brain is an organ just like every other organ in the body and it, too, can become diseased. The brain is more tangible than the term "mental." If doctors cut into our skulls during brain surgery, they can touch it. It's as real as the hands in front of our faces. My advice to those who feel shame and are scared to let people know of their brain health condition: be bold, be true, and never again silence your pain. Your pain is valid; your pain is worthy of my time and that of others; and your pain matters simply because you do. You are worth it so don't hold back, no matter the reactions and misperceptions of others.

If you told me as I laid there, post-surgery in a bracing structure, that someday I'd be traveling three hundred plus days annually sharing stories around the world, I would not have believed you. If you told me I'd be spreading messages of hope, healing, and how I live in recovery but am not recovered, I'd have laughed at you and as much as I don't like using the word, I'd call you crazy. If you shared with me that I'd have a national bestselling book for nearly a decade, I'd be flabbergasted. Then a nine-time international award-winning documentary film, and most importantly that I'd have a loving wife, and two beautiful godchildren (Hi Judah and Zoey, I love you!), I'd never think it possible.

Not to mention that before he passed of kidney disease, my lovely wife, Margaret, and I would have and love a cliché golden reddish-brown dog named, Max (cliché because 85 percent of all American male dogs and cats are named Max) whom we adored. Max hated one thing in life: children. Except those we obviously loved, then he was a sweetheart. It was the weirdest thing. We tried to train this irrational negative behavior out of him, but he was relentless. If he saw a child, he would immediately go bananas and lunge. It was terrible and almost got him euthanized by animal control one afternoon when he escaped our home through eating a hole in the fence of our backyard, his sanctuary (or so we thought). We were constantly apologizing to neighbors, neighbors we loved.

This is what I love sharing to audiences everywhere: suicide is not the answer to your problems. No, it is the problem. We must find ways to be resilient in the face of pain. Think about what you might miss before you make that drastic attempt on your one and only life. We are all going to die someday; for heaven's sake, give yourself time and hard work, which will lead to hope for things to change. "Hard work" as my dad used to say, "Because nothing good ever came without it!"

This newfound perspective I gained post jump has been the "director" of my life. I sometimes miss the mark, but most days, I intentionally take nothing for granted. People I meet, places I go, things I get to do. I live with complete intention with everything I do. I often call my strong friends and ask them how they are doing. I ask them how their brain health is doing. I surround myself with positive, loving people, which in turn makes me feel more positive and loved. It makes me feel seen. If I wake up six feet above ground, it's a great day. I know it's not for everyone, and I want to first acknowledge that, but I pray every day. When I awaken, before meditation, before touching my phone, and before my workout, I pray to God. It usually goes something like this: "God, thank you for this gift of life, thank you for saving me all those years ago. Thank you for putting me on this path and allowing me to be a conduit, a messenger to help those with brain pain survive and thrive. I am so grateful to be alive, to simply be granted the ability past the day I should have died to still exist."

Then I throw in three Hail Marys, an Our Father prayer, and a plea to St. Michael to keep my friends, loved ones, myself, and my wife protected each day. If the day becomes difficult, if I have a hard time mentally, emotionally, or get in an argument with my lovely wife, Margaret, I give it up to God and remind myself how truly blessed I am to be anywhere. When I have suicidal ideations, as I often do, instead of letting my inner critical voice defeat me, crush me, or lead me to planning an attempt, I instead contact or go to Margaret and ask for help. Most times when these chronic thoughts of suicide enter my mind, I just need someone to talk to. Someone who will not judge me, tell me those thoughts are wrong, or say I'm wrong or bad for having them. She is my rock, my love, and my light. She gets me through it every time. When she does help me, I am able to hold great perspective in the moment. I can relinquish the ideation, get back to a safe place, and feel ready to tackle all that is in front of me. I believe that perspective and perception are the key to anyone's survival from suicidal ideation. If you perceive that you can remain here, and your perspective can become clear, you will always find a reason to continue. Four key practices to remain alive, and never die by suicide or attempt again are: question your perception; find a positive, and powerful purpose-driven perspective; hold immeasurable gratitude for everything in this life; and learn to be resilient in the face of pain.

Think about this, you—yes, you—reading this right now! You are just about as resilient as they come because you are still here, doing the work (reading this book) to fight for your well-being, or you are reading this so you may help fight for the well-being of someone you love or care for. If we focus our energy on perception, perspective, gratitude, and resilience, nothing and no one can stop us from achieving what already lies within, personal happiness. It's been inside you this whole time.

When you go through what I've been through and come out on the other side, you see things from an entirely new lens. From continuous abandonment as an infant, to the early death of my brother, my adoption, then later in life learning about the tragic deaths of both of my biological parents, to my diagnosis, and my alcohol misuse in high school and college, all the way leading up to my leap from the bridge, my perspective was broken. Yet even after all these struggles in my life, I've chosen to find the beautiful side. I choose daily to find the gifts in everyday existence. I choose hope beyond the pain, and so can you.

CHAPTER 4

The Journey Forward

The journey forward would prove long and arduous, modeling itself after a roller coaster. Constant waves and cycles leading me into natural manic euphoric highs and then diving me into the darkest depths of self-destruction, despair, and depression. My attempt in this regard was just the beginning. The footprint in the sand that started a path I am still on today. I am by no means recovered from mental illness or suicidal thoughts. Instead, I remain on a journey filled with ups and downs, highs, lows, and in-betweens. This forward-moving journey has affected the lives of everyone in my inner circle, my entire extended family, my newly found biological family, all my friends, and finally, since the story has been so public, it has affected the lives of the nearly one billion who have heard, watched, or read the story. I now have a clear and present responsibility. To stay alive no matter the pain, no matter the struggle, and no matter the chronic suicidal thoughts. I intend to do so. I intend to die of natural causes at the ripe ol' age of 112, holding my lovely wife, Margaret's hand, in a hospital setting, drifting off into the abyss, like in the film *The Notebook* that I never saw twice or cried during...*twice!* That's the plan anyway. I think it's a nice one.

I have worked tirelessly for my brain health and physical well-being since my diagnosis and attempt. I have created what I call *The Art of Wellness*. (A book dedicated to the art of wellness and mental health hacks coming soon.) The first thing I do daily is wake up and meditate through resonance breathing. I take twenty to forty deep resonance breaths. inhaling four seconds through my nose, holding my breath for four seconds, then releasing my breath through pursed lips like a whistle but no sound for six to eight seconds. Warning: do not engage in resonance breathing if you have a low blood pressure condition. Resonance breathing, which I have done for years, lowers the heart rate, lowers stress and cortisol levels, lowers blood pressure, quells an adrenaline rush, calms a panic or anxiety attack, and has so many other health benefits. Eighty-nine percent of the population is not breathing properly. They are breathing shallow, short breaths during anxious times, threatening situations, arguments, and, in times, when they are generally upset. This leads to a depletion in oxygen to the brain and affects the brain's functionality.

Recently, I have found the power and importance of a few thousand-year-old form of meditation. Transcendental meditation to be specific. It's arguably the easiest meditation practice to learn. It's something anyone can learn, and anyone can master. This practice takes you to a quiet place in your mind. Transcendental meditation was taught to me by Bob Roth, the CEO of the David Lynch Foundation. The foundation has helped tens of thousands of people transform their lives through this practice. TM has absolutely transformed mine. My relationships are better because of it; whenever I need calm, I engage in it; wherever I go in the world I can do it. Every day is better because of it.

As I grow older living with this diagnosis, I find new tools to keep me sane to the best of my ability. Some of my mental health hacks on this journey forward include the daily drinking of either chamomile tea or turmeric and ginger tea. Chamomile has been proven to lower anxiety and calm stress. Turmeric and ginger are both proven to reduce inflammation in the body, as well as reducing cancer risk. I drink a bitter melon, celery, green apple, and spinach concoction almost daily as well for its incredible energy boost, cancer-fighting agents, and nutritional value.

Today as I embark on this forward-moving journey, I take stock of what's bothering me and I always, even if I am uncomfortable, speak my truth to my wife or others I love. This allows nothing to fester in my head or lead me to perseveration and repetition or even resentment of others. We put all our issues on the table, my family and me. We do not hold judgment; we simply listen to understand, not to respond. As men in society today, we are looked upon to buck up, stand tall, never show weakness, and fear to our closest allies. I think that's all bull#$%^! I share, share, and share some more. I used to hold it all in. That route almost killed me! I will never be silent in my pain again; it's probably the biggest weapon in my arsenal to stay alive. I'm honest to a fault with those who love me, no matter if it's upsetting to them. We then discuss said issue, or matter, find a solution, or if there's none to be found my wife and I have a saying: "Fix it or feel it." If there is no immediate solution, we just feel it together and move past it.

One of the biggest changes in my life has been in the food I consume. I want to first recognize that as someone who has lived with eating disorders, I do not want to shame or judge anyone's eating habits or struggles. That said, there is great research being done currently as it pertains to inflammatory versus noninflammatory foods. Instead of getting deep into it. I'd encourage you to do your own research, consider your own conditions and issues, talk to your doctors, and create healthy eating habits with that in mind. Healthy means so much to so many different people. I've personally found that nutrient-dense meals from whole foods that are also noninflammatory help me stabilize mentally the most.

Therapy, therapy, therapy, wow do I love therapy! Therapy is different for every person, and I am of the opinion as a BIPOC man that therapists need to be culturally competent when it comes to treatment. They need to meet me where I'm at. Since I love therapy, I take it very seriously. Talk therapy is my go-to. I utilize teletherapy regularly. During my sessions, I am focused and tuned in. I listen intently to my therapist's suggestions (Thanks, Dr. Hastik!). I also work hard in the days prior to prepare for my treatment. I write questions down that have accumulated between sessions, and I list out reasonable and achievable goals between therapy days. These are simple but important goals I can knock out before my next visit. Therapy does not always mean talk; exercise is a form of therapy and can absolutely affect the brain and change the way you think, act, and feel. Regular exercise, if you are lucky enough (as so many are not) to be physically capable, can significantly benefit brain health. We know from the University of Georgia that twenty-three minutes of rigorous exercise with minimal rest leads to twelve hours of better mood; do that twice a day and you are looking at twenty-four hours of better mood. Who doesn't want that?! The moral of the story: if you are in mental pain, and need a positive release, get down, get to work, and over a period of time, see incredible #SanityOverVanity results. Make exercise part of your important routine. I exercise three to six times a week, based on how I am feeling mentally.

Alright! Now for a two-parter. Two parts to one step that can help any of us continuously move forward to triumph over adversity. Education. I have traveled on an educational path on the topics of mental health, suicide prevention, awareness, food as medicine, the gut microbiome, bipolar depression, cultural competency, and mental illness. I get Google alerts on all of them and articles and papers on these topics seem to be filling my inbox. I am gleaning all that I can from the scientific community, certain organizations in mental health, and just general knowledge acquired from those like me with lived experience. Then I go forth and educate those around me regarding my diagnosis. That way, we are all on the same page and they can see the signs of brain decline or mental despair and help me before it's too late. Two of the greatest books in my toolbox are *Loving Someone with Bipolar Disorder* by Julie A. Fast and *Bipolar Disorder for Dummies* by Candida Fink and Joe Kraynak. In fact, I reached out to Joe Kraynak and Candida Fink on Twitter some time ago and they invited me to write a page in their book's third edition. If I hadn't survived my attempt and never attempted again, this opportunity would never have arisen. What a gift!

My next step forward in this journey was learning all I could about how to implement coping strategies (a.k.a. coping mechanisms) for my better brain health and finding hobbies filled with positive, productive, and purposeful outcomes. Getting into the routine discussed above is a coping strategy all on its own. Finding new ways to communicate my pain to those around me is key. Spending quality time with top-notch influences in my life is pertinent. Taking walks with my wife is a coping mechanism. Walking my emotional support animal, Max, when he was still with us was a coping mechanism. Taking Max with me on planes to go to speaking gigs was totally a coping strategy. Sketching supervillains that mirrored the pain I felt inside for so long was a coping mechanism. There are so many more, but you get the picture. You must think of and create things that make you feel good, better, and best even while struggling and battling your personal brain pain. They will not only help you cope, but they will also help you stay alive.

How could I move forward without this next one? Sleep is probably one of the most crucial steps to master. It's one of the most important factors to your mental well-being. When you sleep properly, seven to eight hours a night, you are healing and creating brand new brain cells for the next day. Sleep is pertinent for your body to heal physically as well. I get seven to eight hours of sleep between four and seven nights a week. My goal is to sleep soundly most days to live healthier mentally. If I do not get good sleep, I don't feel good. Insomnia is one of the main factors to psychosis. If you live with insomnia, my suggestion is to go talk to a doctor today, not tomorrow, not the next, but right now! One method to getting better sleep is to stop drinking caffeine for the day at 1:30 or 2:30 p.m. Caffeine has a seven-and-a-half-hour half-life, affecting your sleep function for the next few hours. Trust me: I know from experience, I used to have seven cups of coffee or more a day. It was wreaking havoc on my circadian rhythm. Meditation helps with sleep. Calm, soothing music twenty minutes before bed is a great technique to help you sleep better. Maintain a regular wake up and bedtime daily to the best of your ability. I wake up every day between 6 and 7 a.m. and I go to sleep between 10 and 11 p.m. nightly. This has helped me defeat five simultaneously diagnosed sleep disorders. Three years ago, I lived for the first two years with insomnia, narcolepsy, sleep paralysis, sleep apnea, and parasomnia. This caused my equilibrium to collapse, which led me to being both physically and mentally off-balance. There were times I could not read, write, or talk. The sleep disorders led to constant hallucinations throughout the day. It was as if I could not escape my hallucinatory tormentors. I saw what can only be described as demons all day long, every day for two whole years. It was a f%&*@$! nightmare. It was horrifying! The unending psychosis seriously affected my work life, my marriage, and my relationship with my family and friends.

It took years to come back to a safe place, two years to regain my sanity. Not to mention a couple of sleep studies, and a great deal of hard work to shift my circadian rhythm and get back on track. I created this brain health plan shortly after my attempt off the bridge. I implemented it in my third psych ward stay, and I have followed it off and on since then. I've lost the routine many times, as one with a severe brain disease (mental illness) might do when they think they are cured. When I break the routine, I always find myself back in a psych ward. However, I am happy to say that after my last psych ward stay, pre-pandemic in 2019, I have been blessed enough to stay out of a locked down unit for the last four years. Let it be known that I still have all my symptoms, but what I also have is a dedication, drive, and commitment to staying well most days. Today I manage the disease, it does not and will not manage me! It has not been easy, but I am finding strength in the hard work I do to stay above ground.

I take medications for my brain health daily. They help me, they are not for everyone. My meds keep most of my delusions, paranoias, and hallucinations at bay or better stated, and they allow me to cope with them when they appear. Some people have horrible reactions to meds. I've been there—trust me; you'll find out in the chapters to come. Even so, without meds I am unable to function. I ride on manic highs that lead to darkness, and depressions so great I feel I am a burden to those who love and care for me. This leads me to suicidal ideation, planning, and (in the past) actions. Today partially because of my meds (a factor to my wellness routine) I am able to stop suicidal ideations in their tracks, tell someone near me about my pain, and be here tomorrow and every single day after that!

Finally, my last step to moving forward was developing a mental health emergency plan. It is all too easy for mental health clinicians and organizations to repeat that one in five people live with a diagnosable mental illness. It is my opinion that we should be more inclined to teach and make aware that five in five of us has mental health, because mental health is just health! If five in five of us must take care of our brain health, that equalizes us all. We are in this together, literally. The pandemic of 2020 has shown that in droves. With more people than ever before living with severe burnout at work, which leads to situational depression, mental struggles, and so many suicides. We must also look at the teenagers and young adults dying at alarming rates by suicide because no one taught them how to plan for pain.

My ten or so steps to forward movement culminates in my emergency plan so that when you are well enough you can create said plan, then when you are not well, your family, friends, and doctors can work together to keep you safe. None of this is possible without developing a plan. Your peers, personal protectors, and carers can have release forms signed from all your doctors to be privy to your treatment. This way, when you are unwell, they can talk to your docs, obeying yet subverting HIPPA privacy laws, and gain access to how you are doing in clinical, psychiatric, or physical care. This allows for the onus to be placed on those who remain well, sane, and in good judgment when you are lacking in those traits. It will help keep you alive, as it has helped me, and thousands around the world who follow my ten steps to forward movement. Whether you are burnt out, overstressed, paranoid, delusional, living with a diagnosed mental illness, or simply in need of a calmer and quieter life, this plan is right for you.

So, the lesson learned in this chapter on how to find forward movement inside your battles is: do the hard work, put in the effort, and fight for your mental well-being. Work tirelessly for better brain, mind, behavioral, physical health, and wellness. I did it, I do it daily, and so can you. Do not let your inner critical voice determine or hinder your success. Recite, repeat, and believe positive voices; retrain your brain to have self-love again. As I've said, I don't always meet the mark, but the best thing about me is that no matter what, I keep trying. I keep on keepin' on. I win the game of life one day at a time. One step at a time, and they are all baby steps. Trust me, you've got this! I believe in you. Go!

CHAPTER 5

Going Back to the Bridge

Going back to the bridge was the very last thing on my mind on September 25, 2001. A year to the date of my attempt, nearing the time of my attempt. Then my stoic, hard-nosed, white-blond-haired, wrinkled father, Patrick, called me. I was yet again at City College of San Francisco, the same location where I readied myself to end it all just a year prior.

That was the hardest day and moment I had experienced in an entire year. It would also prove to be one of the most cathartic, therapeutic even. On the anniversary of my attempt, both my father and I found exactly what we were searching for. Well, what he was searching for, but which affected me in the same way. That day, September 25, 2001, my dad and I found closure. It didn't solve all our problems or our issues with communication. What it did was create a feeling of conquering the very hurdle that nearly took me. The Golden Gate Bridge...we conquered that S%^&! What happened that day back in 2000 was not going to define me. It was not going to own me. Have I made my life's work and my lovely wife's life's work about suicide prevention, mental health, and building a net to stop the suicides at the GGB? Yes, but I am also completely fulfilled by family, friends, and faith. I am determined to thrive despite my pain. I am uplifted by the stories of others who say my story changed or saved their lives. I am much more than a man living with manic depression. I am much more than "The Bridge Guy."

Every year after my attempt, on its anniversary, both my father and I would go back to the bridge until one day we totally forgot about it. The anniversary completely slipped both of our minds. It was on that day, that year where my sister, Elizabeth, called me and said, "Hi, Kevin."

I replied, "Hi, Lib."

She said, "Do you know what day it is?"

I said, "What? Why don't you know what day it is? Libby, it's Tuesday."

She said, "No, what's the date?"

I still had not put two and two together. I said, "Libby it's September 25, how do you not know the date?"

To which she responded, "I'm at the Golden Gate Bridge, and I just threw a flower off."

After that, I didn't need to return to throw a flower. After that, most of my family found closure too. However, I would return to fight diligently against the bridge directorate, the people who own and run the Golden Gate, to raise a rail or net at the bridge. They fought against us tooth and nail for years. By "us," I mean: families who had lost loved ones to the bridge; my father; my psychiatrist and president of the Psychiatric Foundation of Northern California, Dr. Mel Blaustein; president of the BridgeRail Foundation, Paul Muller; former president of BRF, Dave Hull, who lost his daughter to the Golden Gate; the Gamboa family, who lost their son at the GGB; Mental Health America; the National Alliance on Mental Illness; the American Foundation for Suicide Prevention; Dr. John Draper, founding director of the National Suicide Prevention Lifeline, currently of Behavioral Health Link; my colleague and friend, Dr. Jerry Motto, who fought to raise the rail or net for thirty years before he passed recently; and the amazing Eve Meyer, former director of San Francisco Suicide Prevention, who has also been fighting for the rail or net for over thirty years.

All of us combined and so many more came together to wage a war to stop suicides at the GGB. But this recent battle would never have gained any footing without one thing. That thing was filmmaker Eric Steel's *The Bridge*. The documentary laid the very important groundwork for my father, Paul Muller, and Dave Hull to build the BridgeRail Foundation. It was the BRF that fought for legislation to be put in place to raise funds to build the net; it was the BRF that worked tirelessly on this project, going to every hearing at the bridge headquarters and taking on the sixteen board members who own and run the bridge like no other bridge in America. It's privately owned by sixteen bureaucrats, socialites, government types, union members, and the like. They mostly fought against us for years, but our voices became too loud. I recall one year while fighting for the net where the Gamboa family (arguably the most dedicated to the cause) simply dropped three giant boxes during their three-minute testimony on the opulent board room table in front of all sixteen Golden Gate Bridge directors. Inside the boxes, they exclaimed, were one hundred and fifty thousand signatures from all around the world demanding to raise the net *now*.

An important figure in all of this was and still is Ken Holmes, former Marin County coroner, who used to take in and examine all the bodies washed ashore or recovered by the coast guard. His research into the matter had an extensive impact on the work of the BridgeRail Foundation. Today, the BRF is helping people with connections to bridges, tall buildings, structures, and railways across the United States and beyond that incur a lot of suicide deaths with a blueprint for how to advocate for such change. They are expanding their reach and casting a wide net (no pun intended) to help save lives through reduction of access to lethal means all around the world. Most people do not know this outside of the suicide prevention community, but there are three ways proven to reduce suicides. One: using crisis lifelines or crisis text lines. Two: caring letters (invented by our late friend, Dr. Jerry Motto). Three: possibly the most crucial, reduction of access to lethal means. This means, for example, using gun locks with codes in the home of a suicidal person. Hiding the knives in the house of a person who cuts themselves. Throwing away ropes in the home of one who has spoken of hanging themselves; or putting a net or rail on a bridge, tall building, structure, or railway system.

As John Viduari said in my new film *The Net*, "We changed public policy; if we can do it here, we can do it anywhere!"

For years, people all around the world from all walks of life have seen me speak, watched my videos, or read my articles, and asked me if I have ever gone back to the bridge. Obviously, the answer is yes. I went back annually on the date of my attempt. Now, I go back to do media interviews, or to thank the bridge directors who ended up fighting with us to make the net real. I'd be remiss if I didn't mention their enormous impact and effort in making this a reality. Without their eventual courage to do the right thing, we'd still be seeing deaths at the GGB.

People also ask me quite regularly, "How does it make you feel to go back to the bridge?" They assume that it makes me sick to my stomach like it did the first time. But they are wrong. I look at the bridge today as an art deco masterpiece that wasn't safe, much like what advocate and filmmaker Jenni Olson said in my film *The Net*. It's a lovely bridge, certainly one of the most gorgeous in the world. It's even more beautiful now that it's suicide-proof. Going back to it today is a total gift. You see, my friends, I get to be here, and getting to be here is a privilege and a gift no matter the pain I am in. I love that bridge because even though well over two to three thousand people have died there, no matter who tells you otherwise, its beauty and allure are undeniable. We've fixed the problem. There are not many stories in suicide prevention that have ended this way.

Not many have ended this way and sparked a larger movement to reduce access to lethal means globally. Frankly, it's f#@$%^& incredible! I am honored and so grateful to be a small cog in the wheel of such a phenomenal change.

CHAPTER 6

The Ten Psychiatric Ward Stays in Fourteen Years

My first three psychiatric hospital stays were involuntary. I was forced in against my will. However, the last seven stays up until 2019 were voluntary. I walked into the emergency rooms, head held high, turned to the intake nurse (with a loved one present) and said, "I need to be here, or I won't be here. I am thinking of suicide." Each stay was vastly different while simultaneously feeling the same. The difference festered in those citizens of hope (what most people and mental health clinicians call patients or consumers). Friends, we are not just shoppers at Target or Walmart! We are human beings trying to find our glimmer of hope so we can survive our pain. Those who entered the wards before and after me and ran the gamut of mental health challenge and crisis. The striking similarity in every psych stay I had was the dichotomy of its staff. A clear delineation was drawn in the sand, and staff of every ward I've been in stood boldly on either side.

Like in any occupation, there were those on one side who loved what they did. They loved their job, journey, and responsibility to us citizens of hope, and they were all determined to make our lives better. Those individuals showed empathy and compassion and cared immensely. Then there were those who stood on the other side of that finite line in the sand. They were deadened to their jobs. They were burnt out. Each of them was going through the motions, hating every hour that passed in the wards they served. Those folks made my life and my recovery a living hell. The way I got through it all was to remind myself of what my mother, Debi, taught me. She taught me from a very young age the power of optimism, not to be confused with toxic positivity. No, my mom taught me the art of being optimistic in the face of struggle and strife, something I can never thank her enough for.

This life lesson gave me the perspective needed to both go into the wards and come out better for it. My first book covered psych ward stays up until 2010. Let's dive into what happened before and during my fifth hospital stay in 2011 and up until 2019: five psych ward stays in eight years. Before I went into the fifth stay, I had become terribly manic, paranoid, and hallucinatory. The day I was admitted to the hospital, Margaret came home to find me pacing in our living room.

She said, "Kevin, what's wrong?!"

Apparently, I told her, "I'm going back to the bridge, I'm gonna tie a weight to my legs and do it right this time." My wellness had been in jeopardy for some time prior to this day.

She was exhausted and rightfully so. She reacted, "Okay, *fine*! But I'm coming with you! We will jump together!"

I snapped out of it and said, "No! I don't want you to die; that's not proper suicide prevention."

Her reply: "Fuck proper suicide prevention! Come on!" She grabbed her car keys and walked out the door, got in the car, pushed the start button, and began pulling out of the driveway.

I was yelling, "Please don't do this; I don't want you to die!"

She said, "Are you getting in the car?"

Reluctantly, I did. I begged her, "Please don't go to the bridge!"

She finally told me of her true plan: "I was never going to the bridge; I am taking you straight to the hospital. You are unwell and need psychiatric care."

To get me the right care, Margaret had reached out to her entire contact list to find a good psychiatrist for me. She was desperate to get me back on track. My previous doctor had used me as guinea pig, putting me on two meds that counteracted with each other and made me worse. No one in all her contacts had given her rave exceptional reviews of their doctors. Margaret then had a call with an acquaintance, Linda Kral. They had eaten lunch together sometime before, and during my struggles Margaret reached out. Linda was an executive recruiter. She really liked Margaret and was inspired by my story. M (Margaret) called her on the phone while crying and said, "Do you know any good psychiatrists?"

Linda said, "I know the best psychopharmacologist, Dr. Karin Hastik." Dr. Hastik was not even taking new patients but took me on anyway.

Dr. Hastik educated M early on and Margaret was so hurt to see me go through all of that. She was scared for me, worried, and she thought she might lose me. She finally realized how mentally unstable I truly was. Dr. Hastik contacted Dr. Descartes Li of Langley Porter Psychiatric Hospital. Up until that point, I had worked so hard on my wellness; I was running nine miles a day. I was so well for so long. When all this s#!* hit the fan, Margaret hadn't realized how scary this situation really was. It became her crash course in my mental health. She was there every day I was getting ECT. When I wasn't receiving ECT, she'd come to the hospital, bring me food, and would just love on me. My mom and her sisters, Barbara and Moyra, took me to ECT a couple of times when Margaret had to work. So did M's mom and brother, Kip. For a long time, M was in shock; she didn't know if I'd ever come back from this mentally. She dealt with all of this while trying to balance work and family, and Dr. Hastik made Margaret aware that I may be different afterward. ECT has been known to completely alter a person's personality.

During my fifth stay, I was drastically suicidal for sixty plus days straight. For the first thirty days in the ward, my doctors tried various meds, therapies, treatments, and strategies. For the next thirty days, there was little to no improvement. My suicidal ideation just kept growing, expanding, and had become insidious. Sixty days into the stay, my doctors approached me and said, "We'd like to try ECT, electroconvulsive therapy. We think it will help."

I replied in ignorance, "Hell no! You are not gonna lobotomize me."

My main doc then said, "It's not like that anymore; it's been proven to be incredibly helpful to people with chronic thoughts of suicide." Before he said that last sentence, I didn't know what to call what I had been going through. There it was. "Chronic thoughts of suicide." Something I would learn about and educate myself on for the last decade and some change.

During my fifth stay in 2011 at Langley Porter Hospital, I would end up having twenty-six treatments of ECT. One every third day. Just to be clear, twelve is the normal number of treatments one has. They strap you down, shackle your arms and legs, sedate you, give you something to bite on so you don't bite off your tongue, then shock your brain with electrodes attached to your head. My amazing wife, Margaret, insisted on being present during the first treatment; she recalls being horrified by what she saw. It was not easy to look at and it caused her a great deal of stress to witness. Imagine my whole body being shocked, zapped, and warped even. After the sixth treatment, I smiled, which I hadn't done for so long. After the twelfth treatment, I showed signs of getting better and had a real reduction in ideations. Well, we got through all twenty-six treatments and like a miracle cure, my suicidal ideations stopped for the time. They would eventually and quite often come back in full force, but ever since ECT, I've always been able to manage my ideations and recognize that my suicidal thoughts do not have to become my actions. Since 2011, I have been self-aware of my disease.

M brought me home from the hospital. I had a plastic bag with all my things, I then took a shower. I was singing in the shower. Unbeknownst to me, M had been nauseous for a few days and while I sang in the shower, she was next to me in the bathroom taking a pregnancy test. When I got out of the shower, the pregnancy test came up positive. I was beyond thrilled. I was so happy, screaming, "I'M GONNA BE A DAD! I'M GONNA BE A DAD!" Tragically, after eight weeks of pregnancy, we lost our baby, Jack Ryan. He lived eight weeks in Margaret's womb and no more. We were devastated beyond belief. Every year around what would have been his birthday, we honor his passing and think about the life he would have lived. We ponder what kind of parents we would have been. We've been unable to have a child since. Someday we will find a way to make it happen. It would be a dream come true.

During my sixth psych ward stay just a year later, one of my best friends, Chris Cunningham, came to see me. I was terribly manic, completely psychotic, and delusional. When he walked into the ward cafeteria, which I had grown so familiar with having been in that hospital three times by that point, I barricaded myself behind chairs and a table and yelled, "Chris, they are coming to take me! They are coming for us all! They'll never let me be free again. I'll be locked up for the rest of my life. Please take care of Margaret. If I never get out, you must marry Margaret." The rest of the stay went a bit like that until I got back into my routine in the ward and began to slowly get better.

Right before entering yet another locked-down, old sock-smelling, psych ward stay I nearly attempted to take my life. My thoughts fell to considering walking in front of a gray, white, and black-rimmed municipal train in San Francisco. As these thoughts flooded my broken mind, I thought of what it would do to my wife, my family, and my dearest friends. I thought of all they'd been through with me thus far, and it stopped me in my tracks. I called Margaret and she told me to call my mother and brother-in-law. They picked me up outside of my mental health clinic, the OMI Family clinic on Ocean Avenue in SF. Mom and Kip picked me up within minutes; they could not have gotten there soon enough on what was a bright, sunny day in the city. I was heavily considering throwing my body in front of one of those trains. I could not get the thought out of my head. The hard work I'd done to be self-aware of my suicidal ideations is what kept me from physically attempting that day. They drove me to where Margaret worked; she stopped everything she was doing and took me straight to psych ward number seven.

Fast-forward another year, I was back to the drawing board. I sat at my favorite SF café, Java on Ocean, on Ocean Avenue right across from my famed OMI clinic. I was writing in a new journal. To be specific, new for me, but my father's old journal. He'd lent it to me for the day to write down my thoughts so I don't "perseverate" on them, his idea is that if I write it down, I can let it go. It was a good idea in theory, but in my manic and delusional state of mind, I wrote down my chronic psychotic thoughts. Halfway into this psychotic writing sesh, I reread what I had put down on paper, and shocked even myself. Immediately, I called two of my greatest friends, Joe Hurlicy and Jonathan Davies. Both arrived within a few minutes of one another, and both read my writings and demanded that I enter the clinic at OMI and surrender myself to be taken to the hospital. I had to be taken away by police car. I was thoroughly ashamed and embarrassed. In that moment, I discriminated against myself. The fact is, I asked for help, and I got it; this truly was a step forward.

For the ninth stay, I was in bad shape. Manic, paranoid, delusional, psychotic, and hallucinating. That day my mind was shattered, I was running all around San Francisco and ended up in front of my friend, Joe Hurlicy's psych hospital. He worked there as a security guard for years. I could not even reconcile the things that poured from my mouth when I saw him. He immediately acted. Joe said, "Kevin, I am gonna call Margaret, and you are going to come with me. Come on, there's someone I want to introduce you to who is inside." Joe guided me to intake, and said, "Would you agree that you need to be here?"

I said, "Yes."

Sadly, when I was released the next day, the hospital neglected to contact Margaret; I was still manic and wandering like a nomad throughout the city. All the while M was searching for me outside the hospital, I was nowhere to be found. She traced my steps to her old office buildings at the Lucasfilm campus. When she finally found me, she burst into tears; she'd feared I had ended my life. It was heartbreaking to see her in such pain. It became abundantly clear to me that my lovely wife was living with PTSD (post-traumatic stress disorder). This would later be verified by her doctor.

It would be a whole seven years of mostly better brain health after my 2013 hospitalization before I entered my tenth psych ward stay. We had moved from San Francisco to Atlanta, Georgia. Margaret's mom passed away in 2014 from lung cancer. Her God-loving mother was an incredible woman. She was absolutely the most devout Catholic I'd ever known. Jeanne even worked with St. Mother Theresa on missionary work in the past. Jeanne went into the hospital one day for back pain and learned that same day she had terminal stage four lung cancer. From diagnosis to her passing, she had seven months. Those seven months were the most harrowing part of our journey. Margaret's mom passed away, taking her last breath in Margaret's arms. It would change us forever. I was right next to her, holding Jeanne's hands as she slipped away. We prayed the whole time.

After Jeanne's death, I started traveling this beautiful, vibrant globe speaking again. I was in the great state of Texas for a military keynote. I'd done a few speeches that day and then headed back to my hotel. I called M. She said, "Kevin, I'm having a really hard time. My mom was my best friend. I need to do something to make myself feel better."

45

I replied, "I totally understand, whatever you need." She was herself broken by what happened.

In the a.m., she said to me, "Are you sure, anything I need?"

I said, "Yes, love, anything."

Her response: "Okay, love, I'll call you at 8 tonight; make sure you answer the phone."

I said, "I promise I will.

Well 8 p.m. rolled around, and I was in for a doozy.

Margaret called me and said, "Are you sitting down?"

I sat down and she proceeded to lead into something she was obviously worried about telling me. She said, "You said I could do anything to feel better."

I replied, "Of course, I meant it, anything."

Her response: "Okay, well, I sold the house, handled the movers, rented an apartment, we are moving." I wasn't fazed.

I said, "Well okay, where are we moving?"

She said, "That's the thing, we are moving to Georgia."

I thought she meant a street in San Francisco. I said, "Oh, like near Hilary and Shawn's house."

I could tell she was smirking on the other end of the line, then she said, "No, honey, Atlanta, Georgia."

I responded with, "I need to call you back."

Then, we hung up and I sat at the foot of my hotel bed thinking about my family in SF, all my friends, my colleagues, and the home I'd known for the first thirty-four years of my life. After pondering for a bit, I said to myself, "I go where she goes. She's my heart. Home is where the heart is. Home is with Margaret."

CHAPTER 7

The Greatest Love Story

Margaret. An old-timey name for the most incredible woman I have ever come across in my life. She walked into my life, literally walked in, and changed everything. I sincerely hope this part of my story inspires unconditional and unconventional love in the lives of those who read this book. It was my third psych ward stay, the third and final involuntary stay. I had figured out a way to volunteer for the hospital while in it (unethical, and probably illegal). I was wearing civilian clothes, clothes not too different from those who worked there in an official capacity. When she walked in during visiting hours, I was wearing a salmon-colored polo shirt, khaki cargo shorts, and sandals that fit me right out of the box. She tapped me on my left shoulder. She looked at me piercingly with her almond, brown, sexy, cool eyes, and I was done. I knew she'd be the rest of my life. I also knew not to say anything because that could prove quite awkward.

"Do you work here!?" She assertively and sassily asked. The nurses and staff station were filled to the brim with people working there looking at me like, "What is this little turd going to say?"

My calm, cool, and collected reply: "As a matter of fact, miss, I am a volunteer." I stood there in my hand-me-down Ralph Lauren polo, my multi-pocketed cargo shorts, and those sandals from the give-away clothes closet feeling confident that someday, somehow, we'd be together. Before that would occur however, we'd go through quite a trial by fire. Today, sixteen years married, eighteen years together, she is the very love of my life, my best friend, and the single greatest thing that has ever happened to me.

Two weeks prior to Margaret visiting the hospital for her cousin who had recently been admitted, I was into my second month at the ward. One day, in rolls this kid on a gurney. He was immobile, catatonic. He could not move or talk due to methamphetamines and other drugs. It broke my heart. Every single day, the nurses would roll him into the cafeteria for breakfast, lunch, and dinner. Sadly, they'd hand him his tray full, and take it away the same. He wasn't eating, and I was so hurt by his situation. Every day, during each meal, I would just sit with him and share stories. Any stories I could think of. Finally, after two weeks of telling this guy story after story, my goal was achieved! I elicited a response! He looked up from his normal daze and stuttered, "Jee-zuz-Christ-man-you-talk-too-much!"

The success was palpable: I got him to talk. I broke him out of his catatonia. People were clapping in the background. If I'm being honest, it was just the woman who was always clapping but I'm sure she meant it for me. LOL. You see, my friends, this kid was special. Every day during visiting hours, fifteen to twenty-two members of his incredible Filipino-Spanish-American family would come visit him. It was nothing short of miraculous. No one comes to visit you at a psych ward, trust me as someone whose been to ten of them, I know. Sure, I was lucky enough to have my immediate family, and some of my friends visit, but inside those wards I saw people who'd been totally forgotten. It was heart-stopping.

On that fateful day when Margaret came into the hospital visiting her cousin, I would learn that her cousin was that kid. The kid who could not move or talk until I broke him from his catatonia. She asked me the day we met (thinking I worked there), "Do you know where my cousin is? His name is Edo."

I said, "Madame, right this way!" I then guided her there. I walked her into his room. He saw me, I ducked out into the hallway.

I heard her say, "Your nursing staff is so nice."

He replied, "That guy! That guy is a nutball! That guy jumps off bridges; don't talk to that guy!"

I ran into his room and said, "Excuse me! It was just one bridge, one bridge. Plural, that's ridiculous!"

She then yelled, "He could have killed me!"

She walked out of the room with me and said, "Why did you lie to me?"

I replied, "Margaret, I didn't lie to you. I am a volunteer at this very hospital, I just happen to also live here." I smiled, and she returned it with a smirk and rolled her eyes.

Days went by and Margaret kept coming to see Edo; I was smitten. One day she walked in, and I stopped her short at the door. I said with great confidence, "Margaret, when I get outta here, could I, like, take you to coffee?"

She looked around at the H-shaped psych ward we were in and replied, "Oh honey, hell no!"

Even so, I was persistent because persistence is the key with love, mental health, and psych wards. Her cousin got out of the hospital before me. Then I got out a few weeks later to go and stay in a halfway home for the mentally ill. The second I had done my probationary period (thirty days of treatment in the home), I called Margaret. I'd gotten her number from her cousin. This was the extent of the call we had.

"Hi, Margaret."

She said, "Hello?"

I replied, "It's Kevin."

Her response: "Kevin who?"

My retort: "Kevin Hines."

Her response: "Um."

I responded, "From the psych ward."

She then said, "Oh hi, Kevin."

I was so nervous for this call. I immediately dove in, "Margaret, I'd like to take you to dinner."

I had saved up three dollars a day for nearly thirty days for just this purpose. The halfway home took the rest of my social security income. She was reluctant, "Um, uh, oh, I don't know, Kevin."

I said without hesitation, "Oh come on, it's just one date; if it doesn't work out, you never have to see me again!"

She hesitantly said, "Okay, one date. I'll make reservations at 9 p.m. near my apartment."

My quick response before I got jinxed or this parallel dimension collapsed on itself was, "See you then." I hung up the phone over-whelmed with excitement and hope. After a Muni train ride, a walk up a giant, foggy hill, and few hours later, I showed up at M's apart-ment. However, there was a problem. I showed up with a giant ski duffle bag filled with lots of my things.

She opened her door, took one look at the bag, and said, "What the hell is that!?" "Well, Margaret, here's the thing, it's a funny story. When you leave the halfway home on a Friday—it's Friday—and you go out past 9 p.m.—you made reservations at 9—you kinda can't come home until Monday?!"

You should have seen her face; she was flabbergasted. "Oh, hell no!" she yelled outside her front door. "Margaret, I will literally use my bag as a pillow and sleep on those stairs in the rain if I have to, but we have to go on this date, I came all this way." Then I smiled the biggest smile of my life up until that point.

M looked at me and said, "Oh God, fine!" I put the bag down in her apartment hallway and we made our way to Café Sport, an old mafia hangout turned popular restaurant. It's like any other restaurant in SF. They look at you, judge you, and order for you. You best not have any allergies. I have lots of allergies.

Down her hill we went, into the restaurant, where we were immediately seated. The tables were tiny; we were elbow to elbow with all the other patrons. We could hear everyone's conversations verbatim. The host had a total bias. He'd seen M there with her previous boyfriend many times. He even ordered her favorite Italian meal, eggplant parmesan, but the dude didn't like me. I was the new guy. He ordered me a huge plate of spaghetti, topped with a mountain of marinara sauce and a gigantic, uncracked lobster! On the plate was an oddly cut lemon wedge (like on purpose), and a small votive burning with a metal plate above it with boiling butter. That host had given me the most expensive thing on the menu. I was freaking out. There was no way the three dollars a day I received for nearly thirty days could cover this meal.

Our meals came; I was in total panic mode. I was wearing my only good white shirt that I'd bought at Old Navy on the clearance rack for five dollars; that's a two-day shirt. I feared getting anything on the shirt. If I did, she'd think I was a slob. Well, the inevitable happened. I went to crack the lobster. I placed it on the tail, pressed it together, and wham! Marinara sauce all over my only good white shirt. It was like I manifested this nightmare to begin. Things only got worse from there. An inner dialogue started. I said to myself, *Do something classy right now. What does that mean, Kevin? I don't know, figure it out.* All the while, I was wiping the sauce clumps from my shirt and leaving an incredible stain for everyone in view to see. Without thinking, I grabbed the lemon wedge, and I squeezed that lemon, harder than a lemon wedge has ever been squozen! That's a real word—don't look it up. I then watched, horrified, as a stream of lemon juice from the wedge flew like a miniature firehose across that dumb tiny table in that stupid restaurant, and directly into Margaret's left eye.

My panic turned into fear. Fear that she'd never go on another date with me again. But let's not stop here: it gets worse, way worse. In my freakout, I went for the plate with boiling butter. The idea was to place some butter on the lobster inside the crack I'd made. The result was less than stellar. I reached for the butter with the same shaky hand that destroyed the lemon; I tipped the plate and had to watch helplessly as the butter droplets flew across that table, in between Margaret's blouse and landed on her chest, burning her terribly. She screamed bloody murder! The entire restaurant stopped cold. You could hear silverware being put down and crashing into plates. It felt like the music stopped. In my mind, I knew I had to act fast. Of course, that prevented any critical thoughts from forming in the process. As a gentleman, I reached over with my napkin and began wiping the butter away. Yes…wiping butter off a woman's chest on the first date.

She looked down and yelled, "What the hell are you doing!?"

I replied, "I have no idea! I have no idea what I am doing."

Then M did the unthinkable: she said the only two words you don't want to hear on a first date in the first ten minutes of getting your meal when you haven't eaten your food, "Check please!"

I f*&%@! the whole thing up. We were never gonna get married, we were never gonna have kids, and we would never have the dog named Max like I had envisioned. He would be a Shar Pei—with all those wrinkles, he'd look just like my dad. The reality set in; I'd never have the life I had been hoping for with Margaret. Or so I thought. We headed back to her apartment. She walked a mile in front of me, like "I've never met that guy!"

We arrived at her apartment, she opened the gray front gate, and she took one look at my duffle bag. She turned around and in a nerve-wracking voice she said, "Kevin, we are going to the roof!"

I replied, "Margaret, are you going to throw me off?"

She shook her head no. We entered a rickety ol' elevator, went up to the roof, and there were two yoga mats and a box garden. There was even a full moon in the night sky above us, and it illuminated the San Francisco Bay Bridge. It was magical.

M and I laid down on the yoga mats and she turned to me again and said, "So, tell me your story." She was asleep within five minutes. We slept on the roof, woke up around 6 a.m., and we spent the weekend together. What started awkwardly became something astoundingly beautiful. On our second date, heading home from what was supposed to be seeing Mos Def in concert (he never showed, by the way), I turned to M and said, "Margaret, there's something I have to tell you."

"What is it, Kevin?"

"Margaret, it's really important; I'm not sure how to tell you."

"Just spit it out. What's going on?" She asked.

My reply, after a long pause: "Margaret, I love you!"

She was driving at ten and two. She looked over to me several times before uncomfortably blurting out, "Thank you."

Even so, we've now been together for almost two decades, and married for close to that. As I said in the dedication of this book, she is my greatest gift, the best thing that ever happened to me, and my best friend. I'm thankful for her presence every moment of every day. That doesn't mean we don't fight, have struggles, or even that my mental illness doesn't come into play. It means we can get through anything; we are dedicated to one another for life, until death by natural causes do we part.

CHAPTER 8

The Good Wife, Keeping the Faith, and Lindsey Dunbar

The good wife, scratch that, the greatest wife who's ever lived is none other than my Margaret. She has fought my mental struggles to keep me sane; she has battled alongside me when my physical health had me close to death. Margaret has stood in my way, up against the door, blocking me from attempting to take my life again and again. What she's never ever done is give up on me. Even when a poorly thought-out medication change led me down the dirt path to anhedonia, where I became numb to life, numb to love, and found myself hating all things. Even when that fell in place, and I gave up on my heart, my love for anyone or anything, when I no longer felt love for the person in my life who meant the most, my lovely Margaret, she ignored my pleas for separation and divorce, and she pushed forward. She never once gave into my cries and was right there for me when I finally came out of this manic anhedonic state. She is my rock, my soul, my everything.

The faith I hold dear in God, my family, my heart, and in myself are unbreakable. It has always been faith, family, and friends who have gotten me past my pain, my torment, and my deepest inner struggles. Those three F's have guided me along this life to success, hope, healing, and recovery. I don't go to church every Sunday, but I try. Margaret and I pray every single waking day, and we pray every single sleeping night. That's our prerogative; we don't and won't push our faith on anyone else. If you don't have faith in God, have faith in yourself, the human condition, and in your ability to survive pain. In surviving pain and keeping myself on this planet no matter the regular suicidal thoughts, I've gained a handful of close new friends. One such friend is a woman named Lindsey Dunbar and I met…well, I'll let her tell the story.…

Being Lindsey Dunbar

Just over three years ago, I suffered my first of four consecutive pregnancy losses, and I think I speak for most women when I say there's nothing or no one in this life that can prepare you for the type of pain and grief associated with this type of loss. I also think, like most other women, we go into wanting to start a family and assume that nothing like this is going to happen. Unfortunately, because our society doesn't talk about this topic nearly enough, my husband and I went into this very naïvely. Unfortunately, I ended up being one of those one in four women who suffer pregnancy or infant loss. When I went through my first loss, I didn't talk about it much at first. I didn't really open up about it until a month later. I felt like bottling it all up just made things worse.

Ultimately, after talking about it out loud, it felt like a load was lifted off my shoulders. It made the pregnancy I did have more real. Although it had happened, I knew I was supposed to have a baby. Even though it was an early pregnancy loss, it made me realize that the minute you become pregnant, your mind instantly shifts into mom mode—every decision you make, whether by yourself or with your significant other, revolves solely around that baby. You do everything those nine months to protect yourself and the baby. You're already a mom before you give birth. Not even four months after my loss, I was pregnant again. I thought, *Well, the first one was just a fluke, so this one must work.* But no matter how many losses you've had, whether it's one or ten, no loss is ever "just a fluke." I wish there was a better way to say that, but with this, I just assumed, given that I got pregnant so quickly again, that that first one was simply something that went wrong with my body—just that one time.

For almost two months, my husband and I were in heaven because I made it past when I lost my first baby. At my first ultrasound, my OB said the baby was measuring a week behind. She said that can sometimes happen, but in some cases, the worst can happen; she told us to be prepared for anything. In my mind, although I was extremely worried, we went home and thought, in two more weeks, which felt like an eternity, we would go back, and everything will be just fine. Everyone around me was saying to not worry and that it will work out. Unfortunately, when we went to my next ultrasound, there was nothing on the screen. At what should've been nine weeks, I suffered what is called a blighted ovum, or a missed miscarriage. Your body thinks that it's pregnant because hormone levels are present, and a gestational sac with no baby develops in the womb.

The scary thing about all this is I felt and technically was pregnant, and everything seemed like it was fine. There were no warning signs that would indicate that I wasn't carrying an actual baby or that I lost the baby earlier on. The sad part about this second loss was how long my grief and pain were dragged out. I, unfortunately, had a horrible experience with my first OB, as she didn't have great bedside manner, and when she was about to leave the exam room after telling us I was going to miscarry again, she just shook our hands and said, "I'm sorry," with no emotion whatsoever. She didn't offer any mental health resources, which inspired me begin working in the mental health field myself. I asked about us going through genetic testing, she said she wouldn't make that referral unless I experienced this a third time. As if that wasn't bad enough, a couple weeks later, after I'd gone through my loss and had to take medication to induce the miscarriage since my body wouldn't do it naturally, I ended up developing an infection.

The medication didn't work the way it was supposed to, and when I talked to my OB about it, she told me to just wait it out and refused to perform surgery on me. Thankfully, my primary care doctor had a connection to an OB closer to where I lived and I was able to get a referral with someone who told me that I was close to becoming septic. This new OB specialized in high-risk pregnancies and performed what was potentially life-saving surgery within two days—without question. I'll never forget when he came to get me for surgery in the waiting area and said to me, with his hand on my arm, "I am so sorry that you're here today, but I'm going to take good care of you." That meant the world, especially given the lack of medical support and bedside manner I had received before this. The dilation and curettage (D&C) was a quick surgery, but the physical and emotional pain after was prolonged. While still trying to heal from not just one but two losses, we wanted to go through with the genetic testing, as we needed to know our risk for having a third miscarriage. It shouldn't take that many times for women to suffer through such horrible losses to get answers. One is one too many, and, thankfully, my primary care doctor put the order in for my husband and me.

We got the results back from the genetic testing and everything was normal. There was a sense of relief that nothing was wrong, but there was also frustration because we had no solution. So, because we decided to take a break from trying for a baby and because we were afraid of it happening again, I began attending grief counseling, and I began bringing awareness to this topic by having conversations with family, friends, co-workers, total strangers in online support groups, and on social media. I was sharing article after article to shed light on pregnancy and infant loss. It was exhausting trying to get people to realize just truly how devastating this type of loss is. So many people have it in their minds that, once you go through this kind of loss, you should be able to move on from it quickly. I think we all know that's NOT how this works.

This is an intense type of trauma—it changed me; it changed my husband. The pain, grief, and all the severe lows I experienced—and still often do experience—are all symptoms aligned with PTSD and depression. Paired with diagnosed anxiety, these mental health struggles feed off and exacerbate each other.... It's NOT fun. A year later, as the world was experiencing a pandemic, I started searching deeper for more answers because we were ready to try again. Third time's the charm, right? One blood test once again confirmed low progesterone levels, which, without those, a pregnancy cannot be sustained. They were low in my second pregnancy, and the medication I was put on for that wasn't strong enough. Another blood test provided results that were consistent with polycystic ovary syndrome (PCOS). It is believed that PCOS can be an underlying factor for fertility issues, but it's not the only factor. There's still a lot of unknowns around this disorder that a lot of medical providers still don't truly understand. I was prescribed metformin daily to tackle the PCOS, and when we started trying again, I was prescribed a higher dose of progesterone. Then, two months later, I couldn't believe I was pregnant again. We thought this had to be it.... I got a blood test to confirm right away and got tested again forty-eight hours later. For five days, I was over the moon and had gained hope again. Sadly, though, my progesterone levels started dropping, and I was going to miscarry...for a *third* time.

My OB was starting to get frustrated and wanted me to transfer my genetic test results from the year prior over to him. He did a little more digging, and he noticed one of my blood markers or anticardiolipin levels were slightly elevated. When that happens, you're supposed to get retested twelve weeks later, which didn't happen. This organization was linked with my previous OB, so it didn't surprise me in the slightest that this was overlooked. My new OB ran the test again. My levels more than doubled, which wasn't good. I was then diagnosed with antiphospholipid syndrome (APS), also known as Hughes syndrome. It's an autoimmune blood clotting disorder, which means my immune system mistakenly creates antibodies that make my blood much more likely to clot. It has been shown to be one of the more common underlying causes of recurrent pregnancy loss, even though it only affects one in two hundred women who experience pregnancy and infant loss. So, we thought, well, this is it...that's what's been causing all my issues. My OB prescribed me a low dose of aspirin to help prevent clotting, to prevent another miscarriage. However, whenever we decided to start trying for a fourth time, I would have to be very closely monitored and have more appointments than the average pregnant woman.

Just like with my second pregnancy, I got pregnant quickly, and with this intense treatment plan I was on, I felt like this was *finally* going to work out for us. At the end of my first trimester, my OB planned on putting me on an anticoagulant injection, as the aspirin was expected to do what it needed to do to keep me from miscarrying. After confirming with multiple at-home pregnancy tests and blood tests and getting past five weeks again, we had a very early ultrasound this time, where everything was looking promising. My second ultrasound showed that a baby was indeed developing, and we got to see a heartbeat on the monitor. Everything was great—I was an anxious mess and literally monitored my every move and everything I put into my body. It was exhausting, but I knew it was going to be worth it. Two weeks later, I was at nine weeks, and we got to see the baby move.

It was the most magical thing I've ever seen. I experienced some bleeding after this ultrasound, which my OB attributed to some internal irritation and me being on all these medications. Until my next ultrasound, I tried to relax and just trust that everything would be okay. The day of my thirteen-week ultrasound arrived, and my husband and I felt amazing, as we were almost out of the first trimester, which was a milestone for us! I got on the table, and my OB expressed his excitement, too, which made me feel better. As he was watching the screen, he said the baby was hiding and that he needed to search a bit. What went from the baby being silly turned into a tragedy within seconds. I can still vividly remember his facial expression, even with a face mask on, and his eyes just fixated on the screen, completely frozen. I knew something was wrong. I asked with hesitation, "Is everything okay?" He paused for a solid five seconds, and he shook his head and said, "No." My heart felt like it sank to my stomach...this wasn't real. I thought, there is no way that this could be happening to me a fourth time, after everything we've been through, with how careful I've been, and being on these medications that worked for most women. The worst part about this one was we saw everything on the screen—we saw our baby, lifeless, with no heartbeat. And when he told us what happened. It was exactly what happens with antiphospholipid syndrome—a clot occurred in the placenta and stopped all blood flow to the baby. My instant thought was that my body let me down...FOUR FREAKING TIMES.

As a woman, when our body doesn't do the one thing that is supposed to be able to do without any issues, you feel like an absolute failure—to yourself, to your significant other, and to your baby. That's the other terrible part about all of this that not everyone thinks about—it wasn't just affecting me, but it was affecting my husband too, who also desperately wanted to be a parent. We wanted to experience parenthood together, and we had been trying to make that happen for almost three years at the time. Because of the complications I had with my second one, I opted to have another D&C. I remember going into the hospital for that surgery, almost two years to the day I was there for my second loss, not feeling scared; this time, I felt beyond defeated, angrier, more frustrated, more confused.

Let me break it down: one in four women suffer pregnancy or infant loss; 80 percent of those women go on to have a healthy pregnancy after; of those 20 percent women who have multiple losses, one in two hundred have antiphospholipid syndrome; 80-85 percent of those one in two hundred women go on to have a healthy pregnancy after going on the most basic treatment plan like mine for antiphospholipid syndrome, which I did not experience.

When you really think about it, I am the minority of the minority of the minority. It can be so demoralizing, as you feel like less of a woman when you see others around you having babies and, usually, no losses—like it's nothing. Often, it seems like they take for granted what they have. It's like a gift—their bodies could do this amazing thing that mine couldn't, and it was completely out of my control. Then I had a lot of people ask me, "Well, can't you just do IVF?" My case is different...I suffer from fertility issues, not infertility. I am not a candidate for IVF. I can get pregnant easily, which seems great, but it's less common than those who have a hard time conceiving, and it's a lot harder to diagnose and treat. I have been doing ongoing research and have read article after article and talked with other women with similar situations to figure out why I deal with this and what can be done to overcome it. I have one option left, but it can be risky.

We're not quite at that stage yet, and we're focusing on other things for the time being, but we haven't given up—not yet. Because I felt like I've done everything to try to heal from the first three, I decided that I needed to try something else to cope with what was the most difficult of my losses, given how far along I got and that it was my fourth in a row. One of our close friends said it best, "One is unfair, two is tragic, three is inconceivable, four is just beyond cruel." Even though I had the most supportive husband in the world and a circle of close friends and family members who helped me, it still felt very isolating. One of the pages I followed on Facebook since my second loss was called Miscarriage Matters Inc. I reached out to them after seeing an ad for their mentor program, and I talked with the director to hear about what a mentor does. I would have the opportunity to help other women who have gone through this type of loss learn how to grieve, process, heal, and cope in healthy ways. Since I was in counseling school, working on my second master's degree, I felt like that this was right up my alley, especially given what I've been through, and I figured through helping other women I could possibly find some peace and not feel so alone in my struggles.

It ended up being one of the most emotionally taxing roles I had ever taken on, but I also learned a lot of valuable things too. I learned how others grieve. I learned that sometimes it's not as easy for people to be open about this sort of thing even though it came so naturally to me. I felt like I was able to make a difference doing this, which, for me, felt like a way to honor our angels. I decided to take it one step further and hold a local 5K to raise awareness around pregnancy and infant loss and help other women talk more openly about it rather than holding it all in and suffering in silence. I also got to do an interview with a local radio station to promote my 5K and tell my story and help others realize they are not alone and that talking about it can be extremely therapeutic. One harsh reality I've realized through this...people are still going to say things that are hurtful. Some of them say things without meaning to be hurtful, while others really just do not think or care. A few "honorable" mentions: "It was God's plan." "There was probably something wrong with the baby." "Well, at least it was early." "It wasn't really a baby to begin with." "You could just try again." "You're still in therapy? How long are you going to grieve over this?" "Don't think about the negatives; you have so much to be thankful for in life!" "Maybe stress caused it?" And my "favorite" ... "Maybe next time you should give up running and hiking."

I won't disclose who said this one, but I will say that it *was* a family member. To this day, these comments still haunt me, especially coming from those who I've tried to talk with and provide perspectives on how truly traumatizing pregnancy loss is. I know that other women still experience them, and I also know that there are women out there who hear these comments and have absolutely no support system. So, I am truly thankful every day for the amazing support I have through my husband, my close family, my close friends, and even my job, which I know is rare for many. My message to all of you is, if you are suffering, and you're dealing with this grief and have no way to be able to process it, don't feel ashamed or hesitate to reach out for help. That's what Miscarriage Matters Inc. did for me, but on the opposite end of the spectrum—I was able to help others, which, in turn, helped me process, heal, and not feel so alone in my struggles. It's corporations like this one that helps normalize these difficult conversations, which we need more of because pregnancy and infant loss is still not spoken about enough.

It begins with the twelve-week "rule," which translates to, "Don't tell anyone about your pregnancy in case you miscarry." Think about it...that's a subtle way of saying that, in case a loss does happen, it should be kept private, which translates into so much guilt, shame, and silence. And all of that minimizes the trauma that occurs with pregnancy loss, making it seem like it's not a big deal when it does happen. Please know this...it *is* a big deal. It's not nothing. You're not being dramatic or letting it affect you too much. You're in pain. There is no timeline for grieving. Time helps, but it will *never* fully take the pain away. The smallest of triggers can cause flashbacks and unwanted emotions, but that's normal. Don't suffer in silence. Acknowledge your grief, and let others know your grief is very real. And, if you have been so fortunate to have never gone through this, know *you are lucky*.

Understand that you have been blessed with a body that does what is supposed to, and I encourage you to listen to other women in your life and their stories of loss and not judge—be empathetic and genuine. Lastly...don't forget about our men—with any kind of mental health struggle, but also pregnancy and infant loss. Men often deal with grief very differently than women, but that doesn't make what they're going through any less real. When you ask how a woman who suffered a loss is doing, ask about her man too. They're trying to be strong for us, and they're essentially told by society to not show their emotions and not feel sadness. I don't know what I would do without my husband always supporting and empathizing with me through all this, but I know he was hurting immensely too. Even through these struggles we have faced together, we've only grown closer to and appreciated each other even more.

With the guilt I often feel about my body losing these pregnancies, he has always reassured me it's not my fault and that his love for me doesn't change because of this. To say I am so extremely lucky to be with someone like him is an understatement. I could easily write a whole book alone on how thankful I am for my marriage, but I won't bore you with all that mushy-gushiness. I just had to make a point and call out what an incredible, loving husband I have. To close this chapter, I want to share my gratitude with Kevin Hines. He is a huge part of the reason why I felt like I could be open about my mental health struggles and not just about pregnancy loss. His genuine honesty and willingness to not sugarcoat anything when it comes to mental health challenges are what allowed me to better accept my own issues. I was diagnosed with anxiety at the young age of eight, and I still cope with this brain illness at almost thirty; in some ways, it's even harder as an adult. Then, you add in depression that stems from this type of grief, a lot of which occurred during the pandemic, which just seemed to exacerbate any problems we were all having, and it's a daily struggle of dealing with two mental illnesses that can be as equally debilitating, but with very opposite symptoms, battling one another all the time. I have been working in my public health job for almost five years, and in that time, I have been the lead on two different grants.

The first one was focused on mental health awareness and stigma reduction and suicide prevention, but when it didn't get refunded, I was able to transition into another grant that had just started, which I was thankful for because I got to keep my job. However, I didn't realize how much I was going to miss doing that work around mental health, and right around that time is when I suffered my second loss and started going to grief counseling. These events combined led me to make the decision to go back to graduate school and get another master's degree—this time in counseling. I came to the realization that this was my true calling in life, and as I write this, I am just one class and a residency away from starting my internship! It's been a long two years already, but I know it'll be worth it. And truly, I would not be the mental health advocate I am today without Kevin.

With my grant, I was able to bring him to my hometown to talk about his story and struggles with mental health and suicide, and through his story of hope, he saved many lives! I am proud to know him as an advocate for mental health but also as my friend. So, I just want to finish my story by encouraging you to continually check in with your loved ones and, most importantly, yourself. Know you are not alone in your struggles, and there is *always* someone out there who cares about and loves you. Talk to someone, and don't suffer in silence. Repeating the famous words by Kevin…be here tomorrow!

CHAPTER 9

The Lessons Learned, and Colleagues Turned Friends

The lessons I learned while in and out of psychiatric units were crucial and many. I learned how to better myself. How to fight and advocate for my own mental wellness triumphs. I learned quite early on that during a spiral downward, with dedication, I could always turn right back around and get back up on my feet. I learned that just because I'd relapse so often and end up back in hospital stays, it did not mean that suicide was the answer. As a matter of fact, it was the opposite. Suicide would never become the solution to my problems because in my world and the world I want for everyone, suicide was the problem. The lesson: living this life until my natural end is the goal. I have learned that no matter the battle, life is always worth living.

In doing this work for the last twenty-two years I have worked alongside some of the greatest minds in suicide prevention, behavioral, and mental health. A great many of them have become the truest of friends. When I was going through my worst times mentally and physically, they were there to pick me up, dust me off, and help me start all over again. They gave me their time, light, and love. They helped me heal. Each of them (and they know who they are) are more than friends, they are family. Most notably, in the year 2003, I met and interviewed with Dr. Sanjay Gupta of CNN. It was his third interview on the media giant's network. We went out to the Golden Gate Bridge, and I (on camera) walked him through that fateful day. We also went to McDonalds and shared a McGriddle. He and I have been close friends ever since. He even joined me as my very first guest on my new podcast *Hinesights*. He's had me on his show multiple times, and whenever I have a new development (like a new book), he's promised to have me back on. I have developed relationships with so many professionals in the brain health field over the years. These connections have shaped my education on suicide prevention and have helped shape my career.

The Meteoric Rise and the Career Path Paved: Speaking—Who Knew?

My father was the very first speaker that I remember listening to. Take a moment.... Who was the very first orator from whom you heard an important tale? One that affected you long after the presentation was finished. My dad came to speak to the parents, teachers, staff, and students at my grade school. He spoke about his meteoric success as an economist and a banker. The speech was held in the old, familiar gym of St. Cecilia's Catholic Grade School. It was the very same gym and stage where the school held its student talent show. That stage, on which my sister and I had both previously performed. The same gym where the church's Sunday doughnut drive occurred. The exact same location where Christmas goods and gifts for family and friends were purchased. So many other events, fun times, and games took place in that multifaceted space—this was the place that the students, staff, parents, and teachers would find each other, share stories, entertain one another, and commiserate.

67

A place that helped build a lasting, loyal community. This ol' fateful gym was the very same place that I would unknowingly enter one evening to hear my father's opening line. It is one I have never forgotten. It is also a speaking technique that I have learned never to repeat. The words he used are against all speaking ethics. Well back then, he did not know it, and neither did I. As he took the microphone, he said, "As unaccustomed as I am to public speaking..." The crowd looked up, and so it began. My father would go on to become a career-day speaker at my high school a few times. When he would finish, his presence in any room was thick and quite palpable. You could almost feel it. He was my hero from the beginning. My friends were so impressed. "That's your dad? He's so cool!" One student even said he was sure he'd become a banker when he grew up. I joke in my speeches that to get a better picture of who my dad was, take Robert DeNiro and the late, great Phillip Seymour Hoffman, and if they had a baby, that would be Pat Hines.

See what I mean? Big Patty's on the left.

Reluctance is where my speaking career began. Can you believe it? I had no intention of speaking to anyone about my visceral mental devastation or any of my recent lived experiences. I had no idea of the power of the spoken word. Frankly, I had no idea the power of the human voice, let alone my own. There was no way I would share the dark and destructive pain I endured due to my brain illness. This disease I was slapped with as a teenager was so far from my reality. I was in full-fledged denial of this thing they called bipolar disorder. It was this pain that led to me to my first suicide attempt at nineteen. I thought post-survival that I would only share what I did among my family and closest friends. I was embarrassed. I was more than ashamed. I had done the unthinkable. I had survived a jump off the ninth wonder of the world, San Francisco's harbinger of death, the Golden Gate Bridge. It was in the hospital, out in recovery, where two clergymen and the encouragement of my father changed my silence. From its humble, quiet birth, my speaking tours would lead to a hearty seven-figure career, which would in turn create a young, prosperous, and sustainable business. One that is now thriving just as I try to thrive mentally. I could never have imagined this would become my life. From my darkest day, as my father has been fond of repeating, "Kevin, I'm very proud of you," something he never used to say. He finally saw that I entered the light at the end of the tunnel. It's been an arduous and pain filled journey, but one I am grateful for.

My very first speech impacted me as much as it impacted the lives my story touched. I was incredibly reluctant to present my story to anyone. My grade school Catholic priest, Father Michael Harriman, came out of a service my father and I attended in our Sunday best, approached us, and said, "Kevin, Patrick, good to see you; how are you both?" I was hobbling around in my back brace and walking with a cane in my right hand. It was only a few short months after my attempt and amid my physical recovery.

Father Harriman looked at me and said, "Kevin, how would you like to come speak to our seventh- and eighth-grade class this Good Friday about your experience?"

I immediately said, "Oh Father, I don't have a speech and I would not know what to say." Then my dad took his oven mitt-sized hand, shoved me forward, and said, "He'll do it!" I turned and gave him *the* look; he said, "You'll do it!" and when Pat Hines says things twice, yah do it. This was the beginning of the rest of my life.

My father felt as so many parents do, that the only way to financial stability and the only way he would safely see me out in the world was for me to finish school. I never followed his school of thought. No pun intended in that last sentence. You understand... don't you? You probably do understand. Maybe that's why you picked up this book, to learn more, to take it all in, gleaning everything you possibly can about stories of suicide survival and triumph over great adversity.

After that speech I would be requested over the next six years to do hundreds of thousands of dollars in speeches. I dug my feet in and paved an entire career path from those keynotes. Today I travel the world sharing my stories and it has become my life's work. I had been turned down by speakers bureau after speakers bureau. They all kept saying, "We cannot put you on our roster if you don't have a book." I kept that thought in the back of my mind. My work had a purpose, it was about finding that cliched, but crucial moment at every presentation. Did you guess what it is? My reason for presenting started to become about sourcing that single person in each audience who needed immediate attention. The person, young, middle aged, or old who was in desperate need of guidance, hope, help, and the promise that eventual healing would come. The job in my head was about keeping that promise to reach at least one person every time.

This was the basis for the work I was, am, and will be involved in. This ideal is pertinent to me moving forward. If I ever lose sight of the goal (to help people) I will turn steadfast in the opposite direction and give it all up. I will walk away. My belief is that if you are not doing whatever you can to help those around you in some capacity, then what you are doing is not good for you. The second your focus becomes your narcissistic benefit, just all about you, it's time to reevaluate your path. It is time to find another profession, one where you can and will give back.

How I Got Started and How You Can Too

In the beginning, it was just me and my abba (father). We searched locally for people, places, and organizations that wanted to hear my message. The idea was to share our collective story of struggle due to my brain illness. We were adamant with anyone who would consider listening. If they could wrangle up an audience of any number, we found a way to show up, and share. From my very first speech, one I would repeat for the next five years, we knew we were on to something. My very first speaking experience was held at the grade school I attended. The presentation was soaked up by the school's seventh and eighth grade classes. From there, a drug rehabilitation center for teens, and eventually all the way to San Francisco's Commonwealth Club and Kiwanis organization. Back then, there was no way to make a living. It was just a time to grind and, like my father did when he was younger, hustle hard. This was a time for us to lay the groundwork to build a reputation, earn a place at the table, and develop a network of people who wanted to hear this message and produce from it much, much more. The message with which we would create a dialog in hope, mental health awareness, equality, and suicide prevention. This was a message that would soon evolve, grow, and flourish, one we could see was changing day to day. My father and I figured that through sharing our lived experience, we would help in altering, shaping, and even saving lives. Two decades and some change of initiative that would end up pioneering the way forward, forging a movement that would allow so many others to share their triumph-over-adversity stories with the world.

In the beginning of my touring, I would search out places to speak or find friends in the mental health field who would refer me. Soon thereafter, once word of mouth kicked in on a rather large level, I began getting inquiries to speak from all around the country, then eventually internationally. For a brief period, I was a part of two different speakers' bureaus, both of which took advantage of me financially. Finally in 2015, I fired my then manager and I went out on my own with my lovely and super intelligent wife, Margaret. She became, for lack of a better term, my "Wifenger."

Today we rarely travel apart from one another. She handles the business side of things and I head up on stage and belt out my solos. I can say with confidence that my speaking ability grew and grew with every keynote that passed. I am mostly a self-taught public speaker. Although, I give great thanks for my way with words to my father, Patrick, my late great uncle, Kevin Joseph Ryan, and my former acting teacher, the late great John Fennell, for teaching me the art of the spoken word. I also will gladly throw some serious appreciation to my mom, Debra Joan Hines, for having me write story after story in grade school during summer break, it certainly helped form my storytelling know-how. Thanks, Mom.

I had just begun, and I had to keep on trucking. From 2001 to 2004, I spoke for suicide prevention agencies, hotlines, foundations, Kaiser hospitals, grade schools, high schools, and organizations all over the Bay Area and California and some of the surrounding states. I would amass based on today's standards over $600,000 worth of free presentations, just to get my foot in the door. From the work I had done in this short period, I got a letter in the mail. I was nominated and given my very first award for these ongoing efforts. On May 30, 2002, I was the recipient of an achievement award from an over-fifty-year-old 501(c)(3) organization.

The award came from the San Francisco Suicide Prevention organization and its former executive director, the amazing, and wonderful Eve Meyer. She would present the award to me at Teatro ZinZanni (a San Francisco circus show similar to the likes of Cirque du Soleil) with a granite plaque that read: "Using his own experiences as an example, he helps young people learn to find new options for their lives." The work my father and I were doing did not need this kind of public validation, but the evening of the awards ceremony certainly helped me recognize the impact the work was having. It encouraged me to work harder, learn more, and find my home in a like-minded group of colleagues, and eventual friends. It also gave me some awareness as to the players in this game and how their approval of my efforts meant that as I made myself aware of the need of such a hopeful message, so would the fields I had just entered: the suicide prevention and mental and behavioral health fields. I keep my roots close to my heart. San Francisco Suicide Prevention and I still work together, even recently. I stay close to those who have guided me along this path.

Why Speaking Mattered and Who Inspired Me

The work was in its nascent stages. I did not know where it would lead me; I just knew I loved how happy it made me. It gave me catharsis and therapy of the largest magnitude. Who knew, folks? Helping others helps you...but you already knew that, didn't you? Pops and I quickly realized what those two clergymen who put me on this path meant that whole time. "Your story can help people," they had said. "Your story can change lives." This is why stories matter. Narratives have shaped our country; they have shaped the world. We all have them. Not just one story, but many.

I am of the belief that we all need them. It is how we relate to others; it is how we define our worth. Stories are the means behind how we describe our past. They show us the way during our present, and, of course, they pave the road to our future. No one has exemplified this more than one of the globe's greatest public figures, speakers, and authors quite like the man himself, the great orator Andrew Solomon, whom I've had the privilege of hearing in person and meeting. He said, "Stories are what shape our lives and set the course of direction in our lives." Keep telling your stories; you might just get good at it. You might already have a natural knack for it. I have learned that even if you are not a great orator or speaker it doesn't mean you can't be a contender. Your form of storytelling could be better suited in the written form. You never know.

The Dos and Don'ts of Public Speaking

I learned a great deal of my speaking technique from my great uncle, Kevin Joseph Ryan. Before he passed, after living a life nearly thirty years drunk and thirty years sober, prior to his developing stomach and pancreatic cancer, Kevin was a longtime member of the San Francisco union, local 856. He taught me about the power of presence. My father and Uncle K had their own very distinct presence. They are what we call Old San Franciscans. Or a tough, sunset Irishman. I always knew growing up that there was a very visible general reaction when Patrick Kevin Hines or Kevin Joseph Ryan walked into a room. It was clear as day. I learned a great deal from both. I didn't learn much from the Speech 101 class I took and barely passed at City College. I learned what effect a powerful presence had on others the same way I've learned every other major life lesson in this life. I gleaned it from experience.

A Damn Good Read!

The greatest speaking book I ever come across is a book I've read a lot; it is not a public speaking book at all. It's a performance guide for trial lawyers. The title is *The Articulate Advocate* by Marsha Hunter and Brian K. Johnson. That book changed the game for me. I learned what to do when addressing a crowd or audience. More importantly, I became educated in what not to do. I learned from my father and my great uncle who both constructively criticized every single one of my speeches they attended, which was many, many speeches. They would break them down to what worked, what played well, and most importantly what I needed to get better at.

They would let me know what failed, and what I needed to ax completely. They helped me make my presentation clear, concise, poignant, and powerful. The question became not who in the audience could I relate to my story. The better question became whom I was missing. Was I relating to the majority and how could I connect with the ones I had clearly missed? As the presentation evolved and I became a better storyteller, I evolved personally. My ability to empathize has been amplified by leaps and bounds. Without the ability to be empathetic and compassionate with every person I meet, I fail. If you cannot do the same with all of those in front of you, and I mean everyone, you cannot serve the people you are sharing your truth with. If you lack the wherewithal to put yourself in everyone else's shoes, you should walk away from becoming a speaker. No matter the stories of those who sit in the theater or hotel ballroom or university bleachers before you, if you cannot find a way to connect and empathize this life's work is not for you.

Know your audience. Who sits in front of you? What is your audience's demographic? What are their likes and dislikes? What defines them? How do they define your message? How will you relate to as many people in each audience as possible? When you are booked for a presentation, it is imperative that you know these things. It is important that you know everything you can about who the audience members are and what makes them tick. If you don't know this, you are doing yourself a great disservice. If you don't do your homework, you will lack connection with the minds and hearts of those you are addressing on any given day.

Been Through It All? It's Okay: Me Too!

Why do we gravitate toward those who have been through it all, those who say they have a lived experience? Patrick J. Kennedy said, "People say the words lived experience as if it's something no one else has." As if it's some secret recipe only for the few, but everyone has it on some level or another. It's not unique. What makes someone different from the pack is what a chosen few choose to do with that lived experience. When a group of people from around the world form an alliance of those with such experiences to change the world, that's when it gets exciting. That's when we realized in suicide prevention that the tides have begun to turn. I am proud to be the founding member of this banded group of miraculous misfits. I am glad to be the founding member of #TeamRippleWorld, a combination of nearly super-powered beings, a collective of force-multiplying titans, ready to give back to people on a global scale. These beautifully, amazing characters whose true stories make up the chapters in this book are life changers, mind growers, and just all-around awesomely, cool cats. They care so much for their fellow man, woman, and child that it is something to be seen when they are all in action.

Each of them has one or more intensely painful experiences with suicide. All of them are willing, ready, and able to share their stories with the world so that those who listen may choose a different trail, the one that allows them to live. Sharing messages of hope and healing, with the notion that recovery is not only possible, but plausible is our mission. We know that with hard work and dedication to our overall health, we can achieve any goal. We can achieve it together.

Your story matters as much as mine. There is a tremendous fear of people with amazing stories. It is how those stories are told that makes all the difference. Not every person can be or even become a great orator. Yes, everyone has a story. The messaging within the story must be powerful, moving, efficient, and robust. I learned over time a lesson that was quoted by a friend of mine, Vanita Halliburton. She once said, "A great public speaker must not waste one word." For the first six years of my speaking career, brand development wasn't profitable. I had to have one or even two other day jobs.

I had to establish myself in a field in which I had and still have no proper degree or training of any kind. Given such a challenge, I worked each day to do so. In that sixth year I was picked up by a speaker's bureau whose founding member was Tipper Gore, that she founded while her husband was vice president. It was something I had to audition for. It was exciting. Something I believed would surely take me forward. I was right. Some of the work, and connections through this organization, helped propel me onward and onto the next level.

A second speaker's bureau would follow. A manager would take over the business side of things. I learned a fair bit about how not to treat people. Yes, connections were made, but 99 percent of my business was coming from being out in the field and meeting so many people and organizations over the last ten years. Word of mouth was in my favor. The manager at the time was feeding off my already made connections. The fact is that when my wife and I circled back to each presentation, something was off. I learned fast after having to let go of my management due to integrity issues.

We learned that no solicitation had been done on my management's part; the influx of work was coming from people telling other people that I was a presenter worth booking. The decision to do it myself was easy. It had just taken a harsh life lesson to realize that between my very overqualified and capable wife and I, we could do all the booking stuff ourselves. Why turn it over to anyone whose trust was questionable at best? I had already put in five years too long with this group. The relationship had become toxic, and I was strong enough even after the emotional abuse to move on.

I cannot thank my lovely wife enough for giving me the strength to stand on my own two feet, surely with a major leg up from her.

Margaret has always given me strength; as they say, she is my reason for reason, my true gift. I could not have done any of this without the one, the only, the greatest love, Margaret Hines.

Poignant, Powerful, and Not Pontificating

Are you preaching or are you teaching? You should ask yourself this question during every presentation, keynote, or speech. When you know the answer, adjust accordingly.

Hard Work: There's No Substitute

People's attention spans are less than pathetic these days. They want things now; they can't wait for due process anymore. Hell, they can barely wait for their food to be delivered before they call and check on the order. We want to work fast, eat fast, play faster, and if we're not using the latest fad diet to lose weight exponentially faster than the next guy or girl, well, we mustn't be doing it right. Just look at the YouTube short video or Vine video craze. Useless, mindless chatter is filling our kids' brains; watching a feature film is almost too time consuming for some generations. This attitude or way of life thanks to the "uberfication" of existence these days drives me bananas. Whatever happened to good ol' hard work? Diligence, dedication, and drive—the three D's. Don't forget the one R: research! It used to be that those were valued most. But now, making the quick buck and moving onto the next is what's getting people to break bread. I didn't become one of the most sought-after speakers in my respective fields, or a prolific, in-demand storyteller overnight; it took a great deal of effort and time.

When established, how does one transform their platform? Speaking is a funny career choice. Most people don't even comprehend why or how you can make a living from traveling and talking aloud in front of people. They just don't get it. People ask me all the time. "So, what else do you do?" Or they say, bewildered, "You do this for a living?" Or, "Is this your only job?" They simply cannot compute that I run around on airplanes, land, head to a venue and tell stories, then *get paid* for it. "Whaat?" Their baffled expressions say as they stare in wonderment. What they don't comprehend is that to become a bona fide public speaker, it takes years to develop a platform worth hearing. To engage a group or demographics of people, become in high demand, and have bookers the least bit interested in helping to put you on the map. All of this, unless you are ridiculously lucky, takes arduous effort on the storyteller's part. Transcending from one or two main topics of "expertise" into a new platform or speaking topic, that's a work in itself. Transforming or adding to your platform takes the willpower of ten men to transcend your message and create an entire new perspective on an entirely different subject or subjects; you must educate yourself to no end. You must reach the new audience, or you won't make it two steps into that transitional door.

Staying Relevant: How Is It Done?

How does one stay relevant in an ever-changing landscape? The world is changing; your topic or topics are always growing, forever adapting. Staying hip to current events in your respective field is key. If you fall behind on what's right now, your audience will know and you will be left behind.

Dinner with Friends

Your message must be crucial to who and what you are. The message you hold dear can become a driving force in your life. If you talk about the way of life that you hold dear, you better practice such activity in your off-the-pulpit time. Your true passion has to be to change the status quo. There's nothing wrong with that. That said, it's imperative to know when to shut it off. It's one thing to be asked a direct question about your work. It's another thing to let those conversations arise unprovoked and take over your daily narrative. Try to remember your friends, family, and even colleagues have lives outside of your speaking world, and want to engage in all kinds of worldly issues and are not necessarily interested in a twenty-four seven conversation with you talking the entire time. I've had to remind myself of this more than once. Hell, I've been reminded by others to zip it and talk about something other than the topics I focus on in my speeches or in my work life. Speaking publicly and talking are two very different things. I have learned to find my inner conversationalist. To be a well and even-keeled member of this multifaceted society, I must engage in the wants, needs, and interests in varying topics, and current issues of those around me. Time with friends, unless directly asked or prodded for, is not my inner personal time as a public speaker. Some of these people have been around for a while; they knew me before this visible shift in identity. It's important we do not let our work define who we are. It's important we hold onto who we were from the very beginning. It's also very essential to hold onto those who have helped shape us. That way, we are remembering where we came from and how we got here in the first place.

The Common Denominator of Pain Is Triumph Over It

We have all struggled; if you've lived long enough to experience pain, you have struggled with something. Maybe you have struggled with many somethings. If you love someone who is battling any kind of illness, mental, physical, intellectual, or otherwise, you've been through some s#*%! Whether you've come out on the other side of that battle hopeful or deep into the opposite, into a kind of regressive darkness, depends on the kind of perspective you've kept all this time. Clearly by peering into the lifestyles, decisions, and situations of various people all over the world, some people's current state of mind grows from wretched pain.

There are others who succumb to the unbridled pain and subscribe to their own suffering. This path ends up shaping the rest of their miserable time on earth. That's why I say suffering is a choice. It's not the only option. Of course, there are exceptions to the rule. We must not forget or ignore the rate of abuse and neglect in this world, or even those who have been victims to horrific crimes. Suffering then, and in some other situations, can be very real. Even so, there are those who always seem to triumph over their adversities. I have and I know that you can too. It truly does become a matter of perspective, and how you see the world. How you see yourself. Your daily narrative is widely based on your state of mind. Are you a pacifist, a pessimist, an optimist, or even an überoptimist? Or do you just hate life and all that exists around you? These perspectives are the various realities for so many. But with a shift in your perspective comes a shift in your reality; remember that. I was all of these at one time or another in my life. Being one type doesn't mean you cannot change. I put my feet down, and in the darkest of hours decided to change my outlook. I forced a change to my state of mind. Today, no matter the pain I live through daily caused by my severe brain disease (mental illness), I remain an optimist. No longer is my glass half empty, half full—my glass is toppling over with love, passion, drive, hope, and optimism. It's something I choose. My optimistic mother taught me that. She did that without ever saying it aloud. Watching her get through some of her most difficult days with a smile and the energy of a meerkat showed me how I could choose to behave and gave me an appreciation for life that I cannot deny. Today, in the darkest of times, I remain optimistic because I look at every single decision and experience one at a time. By living this way, I can always find hope. Even when I feel it's not there. I make a promise to myself: "Hope exists at the end of this dark time. I must keep moving forward to find it." With this outlook on life, I can always find success. With this perspective, I can fight for that light, that hope. This state of mind is created from the inside out.

Stories to Learn From

Throughout your public speaking journey, there is one thing you will find more obvious and amazing than anything else. That one thing is a phenomenon with a global reach. You'll very soon have the realization that once you tell your story, you are unknowingly giving so many the courage and permission to tell theirs. It will be life-changing. I encourage you to develop some serious active listening skills. Far too often in life we are not listening to those who are talking to us. Not actively listening. Not learning, not empathizing, and, frankly, not caring. We humans are far too self-absorbed and are truly just waiting for the other person to stop talking so we can say what's on our minds. We are thinking about what, and how we will respond. Which life story can we recite that tops or overshadows the person who is striving for our uninterrupted attention? Attention we are failing to give adequately due to a lack of interpersonal skills, and the flourishing nature of disconnected connectedness. When you share your pain, your stories, and your experiences on such a large stage, people inevitably find hope in their stories; they relate, and they reveal all. It is my absolute favorite part of this line of work. I get to hear from people in every continent, either face-to-face or from the written word. It allows me to reach people in situations that would otherwise be impossible. It's a gift in the truest sense of the word. The more intensively you listen, the more you engage through listening, the more you will learn, and be able to transform such skills into widening your reach.

When you let everyone else in the room speak before you respond, you get the gift of knowing what they are thinking, planning, or wishing. When you do that, truly listen to those around you,

you can do a great amount of good in the moments when all others are finished sharing their truths.

If you are looking to blossom into a great public speaker, don't skip the work it will take for you to rise to the occasion. I am wishing you nothing but the utmost success, and longevity with your chosen field(s). You've got this…. Go for it!

CHAPTER 10

Being Ashley Hunt

Inspiration can come from anywhere, and, of course, anyone. This next story is written by Ashley Hunt. She's a great friend to Margaret and I, and someone I have gone on tour speaking with before. Her story blew me away when I first heard it. I was and continually am thoroughly inspired by her words, her story, her wisdom, and her infinite strength. Her voice is powerful and must be shared. She's also got a few great steps to well-being that could just be some much-needed answers for some of you reading.

Ashley Hunt

One thing I know to be true about this life is that it can be summarized into a bunch of moments that define and redefine your journey. Moments that impact you momentarily and others that change the trajectory of your path forever. I have had many wonderful moments that are imprinted in my brain, and two moments that changed everything. One being when my mom passed away when I was seventeen, and another when I was sexually assaulted by a college acquaintance at nineteen years old. In both moments, my entire life and identity changed. Over the last eleven years I have been on a healing journey and have picked up some tools along the way. Some call it wellness and others call it healing, but for me they go hand in hand. Wellness is just my continuous journey to getting to know me and evolving into the best person that I can be. This story—my story—is about my personal journey from trauma to recovery and what wellness is defined as for me today, and how my journey continues to evolve.

Growing up, my mom was my idol. She was strong, beautiful, and kind. She had a way of being able to look at someone and make them feel like they were the most special and beautiful thing she had ever seen. She taught my sisters and I the importance of giving back and helping others. She was always volunteering at church and Meals on Wheels and donated blood religiously. She had the biggest heart and a smile that could light the darkest room. She was the definition of unconditional love. She truly believed in me and in anything and everything I wanted to do. If I had a dream, she would say, "Make it a reality." She was truly the strongest woman we knew. But sadly, even the strongest, most beautiful humans can have their own set of struggles.

My mom struggled with addiction and with her mental health. We understand that addiction is a complex disease and is lifelong. But we sadly do not fully know the other contributing factors that impacted or caused her disease. My mom always took on a lot and was very private with her feelings. She did not talk or open up a lot about what was going on inside and things would build up over time. I wish we knew more about what she was struggling with so we could have understood her and her struggles better.

I experienced firsthand the impact that mental health and addiction can have on a person and their family members. My mom went in and out of rehab throughout my entire adolescence, and the time between rehab would vary. There were a few years that she seemed to be consistent and sober, but the last three years of her life felt like every relapse was worse. Each time, the bounce back would be much harder and much briefer.

Addiction is a disease that can bring out the worst in people. It can make the most honest, kind, and loving person the complete opposite. After my parents separated, my mom verbally abused me to the point of me contemplating suicide at the age of fourteen. Now at thirty-one, it is clear why she did. In her mind, if she lost me, she would not only lose me, but my younger sister as well. She would ground me every time I was at her house. Looking back I think it made her feel safe and secure knowing I couldn't go anywhere. But the more she put me down, grounded me without reason, and took away all forms of communication, the more she pushed me to think I didn't have any way out.

Like anyone, I had a breaking point, and after a few years of trying to cope with my mom's struggles, I finally reached it. My boyfriend at the time was over one night and the day had gone the same way as most. She picked me up from school and automatically there was an argument that ended with me being grounded. She took my phone and I was stuck in my room the rest of the day. This time, though, my boyfriend was allowed over for a little while. Toward the end of the night, she came into my room and started to yell at me for something I cannot recall anymore. I was hysterical and was apologizing over and over. She kept yelling and pointing her finger in my face. At one point, my boyfriend stepped in and said, "Kathy, that is enough." He had known it was bad, but he had no idea it was that bad. It was that night that I told him that I could not live like this anymore and wished I would not wake up tomorrow. He freaked out and told me to never speak like that again. After that conversation, I didn't allow my mind to go there. But it was in that instance that I knew something needed to change.

It was after this that my younger sister and I eventually moved in with my dad full-time. Once we left, her addiction and mental health spun out of control. She had multiple stints in rehab for the next two years with each relapse worse than the last. Her greatest fear had come true—we had left her. By losing her daughters, she felt she had no purpose in life. We were her entire world and without us—I believe—she lost all meaning and hope. It was then that I learned how powerful hope and purpose are to human beings. Without it, we cannot survive.

A few weeks before she passed, I went to her apartment. I had not heard from her for a few days and had an awful feeling that something was wrong. My boyfriend wouldn't let me go alone. I told him, "When we go inside, you never go in her room; if I say call the police, don't ask any questions, just call."

When I got to her room, I found her unconscious. When the paramedics came, I was pulled out of the room to take down a report. The officer asked how old I was; I told him, "Seventeen."

He looked at me with sorrowful eyes and asked, "How long have you been dealing with this?"

"As long as I can remember," I explained. I learned that the paramedics came to her address weekly; he knew my mom's address by heart. He explained that we needed to prepare for her passing, as she was not going to make it much longer.

I shook my head as I held back tears.

Next, they proceeded to tell me that she was now conscious and refused to go to the hospital. I tried desperately to convince her with no success. They left and I sat on the edge of the bed as she cried and showed me her bruised ribs from a recent fall. As I listened to her, I looked to her nightstand where there was a bowl of sober celebratory chips. Some that were seven days old, others that were thirty, sixty, and more. I picked one up and started to say the motivational speech I always did when she was in hysteria. But this time, while

I was talking, she started shaking her head over and over, sobbing, saying, "I can't. I can't do it anymore. I'm sorry I can't."

It was the first time I stopped and said, "I know. It's okay, Mom. I know." I held her hand until she fell asleep. I went to pick her up dinner and came back to leave her a note to call me in the morning. I knew that was going to be my last moment alone with her. The following week, my sisters and I went to see her. My dad also made his final attempt to save her. A few weeks later our fears came true. She passed away just a week shy of Mother's Day.

It's amazing that when a person gets that type of news, they can recall every detail of that day and the seconds that led up to it. I was driving to meet my potential roommate for my freshman year in college. We were meeting at California Pizza Kitchen when I got the call from my dad to come home. I knew instantly that something happened because my dad never told me to come home immediately. On my way back to the house, I called my best guy friend. When he answered, I said, "I think my mom just died."

He immediately started asking me questions, but I could tell that even he knew in that instant that I was right. I was sitting outside of the front door thinking I didn't want to go inside because I knew once I did my entire life was going to change. I took a deep breath before opening the door.

Once I opened the door, I caught myself with one foot still outside and my hand stuck on the doorknob. Looking up to the staircase, I saw my stepmom crying and shaking her head and my dad walking down the hallway crying, saying, "Honey, come inside and shut the door."

I still had my hand on the doorknob when I started shaking and repeated "no" out loud over and over.

He took my hand off the door and said, "Honey, I'm so sorry. Your mom passed away." I immediately dropped into my dad's arms, where he sat me down on the couch and my little sister came running down the hall toward me. The first and only thought I had was *What are we going to do with her? How will she cope?*

I remember feeling in a drugged and extremely painful state the next day when I woke up. I never knew that you could feel physical pain when you are in mourning until that day. When I woke up, the only place I wanted to be was on the beach. I went down to the water and called my best friend and talked with him until my phone died. Afterward, I sat there in silence watching the waves and the surfers. There my whole world had just fallen apart, but life was still moving along as if nothing had happened. I was so angry watching people live out an average, normal day when my mom just passed away. I remember sitting there and thinking, *How am I supposed to go to prom, graduate from high school, and move to San Francisco for college when I don't have my mom? How will I live without her? How will I have kids one day and get married and who will tell me, "Everything will be okay because I'm right here with you?" How will I cope?*

After the anger and sadness subsided for just a second, I was able to think about what *I* wanted to do now. I decided that it was time for me to live *my* life and get to know who I truly was. I had given up most of my childhood trying to protect and save her. I sacrificed so much in the process, including school, fun, and even my health. I sacrificed being a kid. I knew that my mom would never have wanted any of this for her daughters. She would want me to do whatever made me happy. She would want me to be my best and treat others the way I wanted to be treated. She would want me to believe that the possibilities end with me. I knew this and that's why a few months later my family packed me up and I moved to San Francisco.

My mom's illness taught me so much and gave me many tools that I was able to carry with me to college. I learned the importance of confronting your issues head-on, and reaching out when you are not okay. I learned that our smallest internal monsters grow stronger and larger the more they are ignored. Most of all, I learned how powerful the mind is and how the body is only the subconscious mind; what we internalize emotionally can be stored away physically. I was extremely ill throughout high school. In one year, I had six cases of strep throat, tonsils removed, and two hernia repairs. I was sick all the time. It was through this experience that I learned the meaning of mind, body, and soul. I learned that if one of these components is off, then everything is off as it is all connected. I learned the importance of a healthy lifestyle and being consistent in that lifestyle. Inconsistency with self-care is just as destructive as no self-care. These tools helped me feel confident enough to move to San Francisco to start over and begin a new chapter. A chapter about discovering who I was and what I wanted to make of my future.

Going away to school is challenging for any seventeen- or eighteen-year-old, no matter how old and tough we think we are as teenagers. But adding my mom's recent death to a new city and new life came with a new set of challenges. Suddenly, this new chapter's learning lesson became about the importance of a support system. I was extremely blessed to have met my roommates. They were my stability and safe place. They not only allowed me to express myself, but they also pushed me to talk about my mom and loss. It was their unconditional and unwavering support and love for me that guided me through the toughest year of my life. Those close friends were my family, blood or not.

Aside from a new chapter for me, it was incredible to also see how much my mom's passing brought my family closer together. We became each other's support system; most importantly, our dad was our rock and foundation. The experience taught me the importance of a support team and the need to surround yourself with people that are there for you through the good and the bad. Those close to you should not get weary when you are not your best self; rather, they should encourage you to embrace the struggle.

My freshmen year was defined by that lesson. It quickly became essential for what was to come next. The next year—when I was nineteen—I was sexually assaulted by a college acquaintance. It challenged me on every level of my existence and shook me to my core. It turned my world upside down and made me redefine who I was all together.

I met my attacker through my college group of friends. He was in the fraternity that my roommates were friends with. We had become friends with this group over the last year and spent most of our weekends with them. Although my attacker was a part of this close-knit group, he and I never connected. Some didn't understand my issue with him. Most explained that he was a great guy; however, I could not shake off this negative feeling when I was around him. A shocking signal of fear would hit me and run all the way down my spine every time I saw him, even at a distance. Something about him terrified me. I would instantly feel extreme anger and fear.

Prior to the attack, we were all getting in a car to go to a party; he was supposed to sit next to me for the ride. I threw a fit and refused to get into the same car as him. My friends asked what was wrong with me. I did not know, but there was something about him. I simply did not trust him. I refused to go to this party. The next morning, two of my housemates told me that I came off as rude. They explained that I did not know him. I should "give him a chance" before I acted like that again. This behavior was out of character for me, which made me rethink my feelings toward him. I decided to give him a chance.

Soon after that night, we threw a party at our house. Something about this night was different. I never left a party or my house without telling my roommates where I was going. Yet, this night not only did I leave without telling them where I was headed but I chose not to answer their calls and texts when they were asking where I went. When I did finally respond, I answered back, "I'm fine." To this day, I don't know how or why I acted like this that night or what my thought process was there. Regardless, I left my house and went with him alone to another party. Shortly after arriving, I wanted to go home. He would take me, but we had to go to his house to grab his keys. We went upstairs to grab his keys from his room. Once we entered his room, we never left. He assaulted me that night, took my phone from me after so I could not call for help, and wouldn't let me leave the house. I quickly gathered this was his plan the whole time and immediately regretted not listening to my instincts and spider senses with every previous encounter I had with him. Yet again, I was isolated and alone in a state of fear.

I finally was able to escape at 5 a.m. the next morning when he was asleep. Walking out of the house, I immediately called my roommate. She stayed on the phone with me until she found me. I remember making a conscious decision to tell her. If I did not, I knew that I would not survive this. I fell apart as soon as I got into the car and told her what happened: "I have been through so much. I don't think I can get through this one."

My dad and stepmom happened to be visiting that weekend. We had planned to meet at their hotel before we toured the city. I had not slept and I just cried hysterically the entire morning. The second I arrived at my dad's door he knew something awful had occurred. Immediately, I told my dad and my stepmom the awful reality of the night before. My stepmom insisted we go to the police to report the attack. I remember walking into the police department thinking that I did not belong here and being so afraid to tell the police officer what happened. The police officer took me into a room and started to take down the report. I started to tell him everything from the beginning. He was asking for details along the way until I got to the part where he began to assault me. He stopped writing, put his pen down, and said, "Let's go. We are going to the hospital right now to perform a rape kit."

He told me he was personally going to take me, and my parents could follow behind. In the car, he talked about how angry he was and that "We will do everything in our power to find and prosecute this man." He told me how he has a wife and that he wouldn't know what he would do if this ever happened to her, and that he couldn't understand how men are capable of such a crime. Once we were at the hospital, he sat in the lobby and said he called in to the station and would be in the waiting room for the remainder of the day waiting for me.

I barely remember the procedure, but I do remember the nurse and advocate that was sent from SFWAR (San Francisco Woman Against Rape) to support me through the process. She was so gentle and sweet. She told me that she was here for anything and everything I needed. Once the investigator came in, the safe and gentle tone that the nurse and advocate so kindly created drastically changed. She came in and already I could tell how numb she was to cases like mine. She was harsh and impatient. The questions triggered my nervous system, making me feel as if I asked for this or I could have prevented this from happening. She explained she must ask these questions, but I couldn't understand how you could ask a victim why they didn't run, fight back harder, or call the police. I remember telling her I didn't think I would ever leave that room and I thought he had the potential to kill me if I tried anything as there was a bat conveniently lying on the wall next to his bed. To them it's just their job and one of the hundreds of cases they take on. Once she left, the nurse completed the kit and sent me on my way.

Six hours or so later, I took a cab home. I kept thinking that I was in a nightmare that I just could not wake up from. I stared out of the window while the cab driver attempted to make small talk. I responded with minimal, short sentences until he finally stopped and exclaimed, "I don't know what happened to you, but I can tell that it was bad. I am so sorry."

I continued to stare out of the window as tears fell down my cheeks. He asked if it was a fight.

I nodded my head, and then he said something that I will never forget: "I always say alcohol doesn't make you into a monster; it brings out the monster in you." This perfect stranger had no idea how badly I needed to hear that in that exact moment. The entire day was I engulfed in such a state of shock, but also fear of potentially ruining my attacker's life and future. The simple, yet powerful words made me realize that this was not my fault. Alcohol did not attack me—he did.

The next few months of the investigation were a blur. After all my mental and physical suffering, my attacker got off with not even a warning. It was a case of "he said, she said" with no physical evidence, despite the kit. I refused to fight for the next two years when the investigator made it clear that there was not enough evidence for a case. The investigation was one of the most brutal processes I have ever experienced. It felt like the law protected my attacker and left me to pick up the *broken* pieces. The questions are mostly directed at the victim and are formatted in a way that blames the victim for the incident. Such as, "Why didn't you run or call the police if you felt like you were in danger?" I lost faith in our justice system during this time and was beyond angry that someone could affect another's life without any consequence.

Shortly after the investigation ended as an utter disappointment, I saw *him* at a party. I walked straight up to him.

He immediately said, "Let's talk off to the side." I refused to be away from my friends and alone with him again.

I firmly stated, "I am comfortable talking right here." I confronted him about lying to the police and our group of friends, telling everyone that he didn't assault me.

He laughed in my face. He laughed, stating, "I don't remember what happened, but I know I didn't do *that*."

I proceeded to quote his exact words after he assaulted me. He continued to shake his head and laugh. I immediately had a flashback of that same look in his eyes. I remembered the evil I saw when he attacked me. I stopped and stood strong as I told him, "You may have shaken me to my core, but you did not and could not break me." Although he may have been physically stronger than me, I would become stronger than he ever could be. I relished the fact that he had to go to bed knowing what he did to me. Yet, I would (eventually) fall asleep at peace knowing he did not define me. Most importantly, he did not win. This conversation has been ingrained into my brain; it was my promise to myself. I promised to fight for my life and future. I would become stronger and wiser through this experience. It, he, any of it would never define me.

With this promise, I thought that I could recover on my own. I didn't need help. I could do it. I was strong. But the more I pushed off counseling, the more I did not confront the issue head-on, the more extreme and horrific my nightmares became, and the worse I became. I felt like I was living in hell. It was no longer just nightmares, but a daily hell—from the moment I woke up to the moment I was going to bed. I wanted it to just be a bad dream. I remember looking at myself after a shower and not being able to recognize the girl staring back at me in the mirror. I had no relationship with my body anymore. I wanted to crawl out of my skin every second of every day for six months. I had no relationship with myself—physically or emotionally. I was either crying or numb. I did not trust anyone, including myself. I was afraid to go anywhere—especially school, as he was there. Worst of all, I was ashamed, ashamed of myself.

Trauma is scary. It can make you think and do things you would never have been capable of before. One time, I was in my car; there he was, crossing the street in front of me. I remember grabbing the steering wheel, taking deep breaths while talking myself out of running him over. I felt that if I ran him over that I might get away with it because of what he did to me. A life for a life. He stole my life from me and everything that I was with no consequences, so wouldn't this be justified? I was thinking and feeling things I would have never thought or felt otherwise. I was so incredibly angry with everyone and everything. I was most angry with God. I no longer believed in a higher being. I prayed for help several times throughout that night and no one saved me. It still happened. If there was a God, how could he let something like this happen to me? How could he abandon me? I truly believe that this shift in my faith led me to my lowest low. No longer having faith in something greater than me depleted me completely of any hope for the future.

I knew I could not live like this anymore. Every day, I was in so much pain emotionally. I was stuck in a prison of a body. Even with my mom, I had never experienced emotional and mental pain like that before. My mind was suffocating me. If I wasn't replaying the night over again, I was paralyzed in shame, fear, sadness, or numbness. It was a darkness I had never known, and what was worse is I didn't see an end to it. I couldn't see the light at the end of the tunnel. Everyone would tell me, "This is normal. You will be okay." I wanted to scream every time I heard those words. They didn't know and they couldn't understand. How could they understand what it was like to want to jump out of your own skin and not be able to? How could they understand the isolation in feeling like you are a prisoner of your own mind, only experiencing feelings of pain, negativity, sadness, and fear. I just wanted to stop hurting. I wanted my innocence back. I wanted to laugh again. I wanted to have a good time with friends. I wanted to be in a relationship. I wanted to love my body again. Most importantly, I wanted to love myself again. I wanted me back.

One major component saved my life and gave me hope—my support system. I was in such a fragile state and all my loved ones knew it. My best friends and family that did not live in the city called me every day to check in with me. Even when I chose not to answer, they would call again the next day. To this day, my dad amazes me with how he was able to support and encourage me through that entire process. It is a dad's greatest nightmare. Regardless, he loved and supported me every step of the way. He embodied unconditional love and compassion for me every day. He always called to check in on me since I was away from home. He patiently listened to me every time I broke down.

But I truly owe my life to my roommate. She literally picked me off the floor several times, played with my hair until I fell asleep, and was the main reason I went to counseling. She was so incredibly gentle, loving, and consistent each day with me. She was the only person other than my family that I trusted. My dad, sisters, and roommates talked with me, listened to me, and gave me hope that it was going to get better. I didn't know it then but being in such a fragile state, I depended on this support and strength from my family and friends. I could not do it alone. I knew the only way to make it through to the other side was going to be with my family and friends beside me. It was through the strength of this support system that I finally made my first counseling appointment.

It is incredible to recall the random acts of kindness that reminded me of human compassion and kindness that I no longer thought existed: the police officer who took me to the hospital and sat in the lobby and waited the entire day for me during his shift and made me feel protected and safe. The advocate who held my hand through the procedures and supported me every step of the way. And the cab driver that took me from my parents' hotel to my house and talked with me the whole way home and so gently helped me get my belongings and self out of the car as he said, "I don't know what happened to you today, but I know and can feel that it was bad and am so incredibly sorry."

I will never forget the first day of counseling, even though it was just a consultation. When I sat down, she asked me to explain the incident. Instantly, I started to cry hysterically. I didn't stop the entire forty-five minutes. All I could get out was, "I am not okay. Please tell me I am going to be okay." I was placed quickly with a counselor. At first, I did not connect with her. She was loving but tough. She saw right through me; my bubbly personality, which I typically used as my cover, was not going to cut it for her. A few months into it, I hated going to counseling. I did not feel that it helped at the time. If anything, talking about it felt awful. I would then leave, and nothing changed. I was still living out this daily hell.

Then one morning I explained, "I couldn't do this anymore." She asked if I had suicidal thoughts. I answered, "I know I would never attempt anything because I couldn't do that to my loved ones, but if I could not wake up tomorrow, I would choose to do so. I can't live like this anymore. I feel like I am being tortured and suffocated every day." I knew this statement too well from the time I lived with my mom. Realizing the parallel in both traumas started to scare me. I began to realize how layered and similar my traumas were. Even though the traumatic events were different, the impact and the parts of the trauma that affected me the most were the same. Feeling helpless, alone, and afraid. I started to fear that if I did not truly confront my issues that I may be on the same path that my mom took and that I could be defined by my traumas.

I knew that I had so much more to offer to the world and myself. This fear became my motivation. I allowed my fear to fuel my drive toward recovery. Even though I attended counseling, I had still not confronted my demons. The next session, I chose to stop running. I wanted to allow myself a chance to become more than my circumstances. I wanted to become defined by so much more. I didn't want to be a victim anymore, I wanted to be a survivor.

I went through a year of counseling two times a week before I "graduated." There were many times throughout that year that I wanted to quit because it was so painful to have to face my trauma. At the time it felt bigger and stronger than me. It was within this year that I learned what being brave meant. Being brave meant that even though I was scared, and it was painful, I needed to face my trauma to become bigger and stronger than it. It was an uphill battle but after that year of counseling, I had gotten to a place where my pain was no longer debilitating and had learned healthy coping mechanisms.

The next few years, my focus was to finish college and keep building up my resume for physical therapy school. I was on track to live a "normal life." But a huge part of me was still stuck in the past. It was as if I was moving forward and checking off the list of what I knew I was supposed to do: go to college, graduate, get a job, get married, have kids, and so on. Even though I was checking off the list, I always felt like a fraud. I was still carrying around this huge secret about my assault. Many of my family members and friends did not know about it, and that silence made me feel unworthy and ashamed. It was a heavy chain inside me holding me down. I wasn't the same girl that I was before my assault and because most people didn't know about it, I pretended to be her. I would smile and be the same little Ashley Hunt they always knew. It was hard to live this life knowing that I wasn't the same person. I knew that if I held my silence that I would allow him to hold the power, and I just couldn't do that anymore. This was when Nfinite Strength, my first company, was born.

After my attack, I learned of more girls and friends who also had been assaulted and a fire started to build within. I was sitting in my bed one day and ran by a website for a retail company that gave portions of their retail proceeds to cancer awareness organizations in honor of the founder's dad. This stimulated my idea around raising awareness and empowering victims and survivors of sexual violence.

I wanted to empower victims of sexual violence. I wanted to build a community that focuses on healing and rebuilding a life after an assault. To me it was simple. It is bad enough to experience something so horrific but it's worse if it defines the rest of your life and future. To grow a community and break the silence, I knew it was going to have to start with me. Breaking my silence meant I was going to have to tell my family and friends before I made it public. Telling them was much more terrifying than the public because I knew it was going to be hard to hear and I knew they may not know how to respond. It was just as challenging as I thought it would be, but I will say that once I did it I felt a weight fall off me. It was that chain that was attached to my silence and attacker that held me down for years. It was the mask that was attached to the chain. The mask that was the old Ashley. Letting go of that chain meant that I could finally rebuild myself. I could finally be the Ashley that I wanted to be. I could start to become the Ashley that I truly was. I realized that it was okay to be imperfect and a work in progress. It was okay to not be happy all the time. It was okay to just be me.

I had recently graduated from college with my degree in kinesiology with an emphasis in neuromuscular science. I had always wanted to become a physical therapist, but after spending a few years working in the field, I realized I loved holistic chronic pain management more. So I continued my education and got certified as a corrective and orthopedic exercise specialist, with my specialty being pre-/post-injury recovery and prevention.

It was around this time that Nfinite was born, and shortly after became an established socially aware corporate wellness company. My business partner, Justine Luong, and I focused our efforts around helping people reduce and alleviate chronic aches and pains while giving back to victims of sexual violence. Through Nfinite, we established many relationships and partnerships with companies throughout the Bay Area. After a handful of local community events for BAWAR, we were able to host our first fundraiser in SF for the nonprofit, Bay Area Women Against Rape that raised over $11,000 with over 160 attendees. To this day, that fundraiser was one of the most incredible days of my life and was truly unforgettable.

After running Nfinite Strength for six years and working with hundreds of people in the Bay Area, Justine and I realized there was a serious need for our programs and we wanted to help as many people around the world as we could. So, we made an application called Pancea, and have been working to help as many heal as we can.

In the last few years, I have been asked how I have overcome my trauma and how I am where I am today after everything that happened. My answer is there is no final destination. I am continuously working on myself and working to overcome my trauma. But a huge part of my healing has come from learning and acting on forgiveness and empathy.

Forgiving my mom, myself, and even my attacker. I have spent a lot of years going to counseling, processing my childhood, and have learned that my forgiveness can come from empathy. I have so much empathy for my mom and the pain she suffered. Being an adult now and having experienced trauma in my life, I understand how hard and complicated life can be. I empathize for how much she tried to balance at all times and for being an imperfect human. I am not a mom myself, so I can only imagine what she must have been juggling. I forgive her for not knowing how to get the help she needed, and I forgive her disease for bringing out a side of her, that was not who she was.

I never thought I would be able to forgive my attacker because I thought forgiving him would mean what he did was okay and it could be erased or forgotten. But after a decade I realized it was never for him. Forgiving him freed me. It took me a decade to understand what this would look like with something so awful. It was an understanding that I may never forget, I will never be okay with his actions, but through empathy I can release my hatred and anger, which at the end of the day only hurts me. I empathize for the pain that he must have endured to be able to hurt someone the way he did. Hurt people hurt others, and knowing that has allowed me to forgive him. My forgiveness came from falling in love and healing through love. I did not want to bring hatred and anger into my future and family. Forgiveness is a choice and it takes time. But if you choose to forgive, I can promise you that your life gets a bit brighter, your heart gets a little lighter, and your perspective changes forever.

Ultimately, I have come to learn and continue to work on creating enough space in my heart to hold space for opposite emotions to exist in the same place. I have learned that you can not be okay with someone's hurtful actions but you can still empathize with them. In my own life, the older I get the more that this has become the norm. There are always tough and beautiful moments happening at the same time. I can be sad about a circumstance I am dealing with but still be grateful for all of the good in my life. When I create enough space to hold both, my perspective broadens. Making life more optimistic and less heavy.

It has been eleven years since my attack and quite the winding recovery road. I look back at those years and the years that followed and empathize with my younger self. Healing is not linear and is not graceful. As the documentary *Stutz* said, "We all have a shadow. A shadow is a version of ourselves that we are ashamed of and want to hide. It's the part of us that we want to deny ourselves." My shadow was a combination of fourteen- and nineteen-year-old Ashley that felt unloved and unworthy. My shadow reminded me of any and every bad way I dealt with my mom and my attack. All of the years I was gracelessly coping and surviving. And it took me a long time to stop hiding her and instead "sit in the room with her." I did this exercise in a counseling session one time and it changed my life. I had to find my shadow and meet her where she was. She was a teenager locked in a room, angry, and scared. In the session I apologized to her for all the years I was ashamed of her. I told her how brave and strong she was for being able to survive everything she did. I thanked her for not giving up and for continuing on even when she didn't want to. I told her I was sorry for how she was treated and told her that she is loved and worthy. And that if it wasn't for her, I wouldn't be who I am today. What I learned is that we all have a shadow and it never goes away but we can learn to love it, empathize with it, and embrace it. I love my shadow and I feel for her. But

I am also grateful for her and who she helped me become. Because of that strong, brave little girl I have been able to attract healthy relationships in my life, fall in love, and am building a family and home that is safe, stable, and consistent.

Life is long and full of ups, downs, and learning lessons. Even though there was a lot of pain throughout those years, I know I wouldn't be who I am today without those experiences and without making conscious decisions to make healthy changes to my daily life. I believe that if you don't like something, change it. Some changes that improved my wellbeing came from what most people think of when it comes to wellness: nutrition, exercise, taking care of my mental health, and sleep. But there are other tools I have gathered along the way that feed my soul and keep me evolving into the person I want to be, such as spirituality, travel, confidence, purpose, and community. The list is long and I redefine and reprioritize which tools I am using depending on what I am going through in my life.

Evolve

Purpose: I believe that purpose can be defined by anything that gives your life meaning and is living outside of yourself. It comes in many forms and can be defined differently for each person. It can be found in your work, becoming a partner in life, parent, friend, family member, neighbor, volunteer, and so on. For a long time, purpose for me came from the work I do. But now I have added being a spouse, family member, friend, neighbor, and colleague to that list, and I know that it will only continue growing. Especially when you are in a tough season, it can be hard to see it or find one thing that you feel gives you purpose. But you are alive and on this planet which means you a have purpose, and it is finding one thing you can wake up each day and do to explore that purpose. Today it may look like extending a hand and helping a friend, neighbor, colleague, spouse, or family member. Tomorrow it may be something different, but there is purpose to every life.

Hope: I truly believe hope is the strongest and most powerful thing in the world and is essential for human beings. And it can also come in many forms. For some hope comes from their faith, for others it can come from their optimism, life experiences, relationships, and the world around them. For me I have found hope through faith in something greater than me, falling in love, witnessing beautiful acts of kindness, and in nature. Witnessing and experiencing love and kindness always reminds me that hope is real and is stronger than any evil or bad that exists.

Confidence and Self-Love: My traumas had a significant impact on my level of confidence and self-love. I talked about my shadow earlier. Another positive effect making amends with my shadow had was that it significantly improved my relationship with myself. By empathizing with my younger self and embracing her, I was able to see the strength and beauty she carried, not just her pain and what she lacked. Psychiatrist Dr. Stutz says, "True confidence is living in uncertainty and moving forward. The winner is not the one that does it the best or looks the best. It's the one who is willing to take a task to act on some degree of faith and eats the consequences." What is funny about this is, if that is true, then even my shadow had confidence. Even though she is and was a reminder of every insecurity I have or had; even my worst self-learned to live in uncertainty and chose to move forward every single day. So, no matter where you are in life, and how you feel about yourself, give yourself some credit and have confidence in the amount of uncertainty you accept and still choose to move forward.

Spirituality

My Faith: My faith is the one thing that brought me back to life after my traumas. It took me a long time to gain my faith back after my attack, but through patience and support from my friends and family, I eventually got it back. It was coming forward about my story that helped me believe in something greater than me. I remember saying a prayer before I reached out to my family and friends to let them know that I was starting Nfinite and that I would be publicly speaking out about my assault. I prayed the day before to give me strength and peace to be able to face whatever was to come with speaking out. I remember feeling so anxious praying that day and not knowing if anyone or thing was listening but hoping for an answer. I knew there was someone watching out for me when I spoke out the next day because all I felt was utter peace. That day my light came back. My life without faith was dark, lonely, and scary. Believing in something greater than you can make you feel less alone and gives you a greater perspective in life and hope.

Community: *We are not meant to be alone*

Get to Know Your Community: Community can be defined in many ways, but for this section, I am going to separate the community into two groups. One that makes you feel accepted and your tribe. We all have interests and hobbies. The great thing about this big, great world is that there are many people that like the same things you do. It is important to seek out groups that have things in common with you such as books and art clubs, improv, cooking, and other hobbies or interests. There are many resources out there that are available to connect you to your community such as apps like Meetup, Bumble for Friends, and Eventbrite.

Get Yourself a Tribe: My tribe may be one of the most important parts of my wellness. A tribe to me is a single person or group of people that you can call on that keep you going through your toughest days. Whether this is a family member, friend, counselor, or support group, make sure to seek out your tribe so that you know who to call on when needed. However, it is important to say that I am equally my tribe's warrior as they are mine. These are people that I have supported and been there for the worst of days as they have been there for mine. It is an equal relationship, which is what keeps it healthy and stable.

Travel

Explore: Another important aspect of my wellness is traveling and exploring. Whether that is just getting out of the city for the day or exploring another country, I make traveling a priority. Every time you get out of your routine, you discover new aspects of yourself and get a new perspective. Seeing something that you have never seen before opens a new part of your soul. In a strange way, nature's ability to make me feel small is the greatest gift of all. Looking out at the top of a hill, mountain, or landscape allows me to see the big picture. It reminds me that I am just a speck in the large scheme of things. Now this does not mean it makes me feel insignificant, but it can help me let go of the insignificant parts of my life and drama that can weigh me down in the moment.

Maintenance

Mindfulness (Being Present): It is tough to be present in such an overstimulating world but it can be one of the strongest assets in achieving peace. Overstimulation causes heightened anxiety and depression because our minds can get overloaded, get stuck in the past, or trapped in the overwhelming future of unknowns. Becoming more present means that we must be in the moment. Not the past or future, but in the present. Practicing mindfulness is one the most important tools in my daily life.

Get it On Paper: Drawing and art can be a very therapeutic technique. But writing has been more of my go-to. It has been such a form of therapy for me (as you may be able to tell with this chapter). I love the quote "name it to tame it." This is a calming technique that can be used verbally to get what you are feeling out of your body and to help release negative emotions. But writing out my thoughts and feelings does the same for me. Sometimes I just write specific words down that describe how I am feeling, and sometimes I write descriptive pages about what I am going through. It's not about having a specific format for me to stick to, it is just about releasing what I am storing so I can move forward and process what is happening.

Create the Habit of Being Present: I am constantly learning and redefining what mindfulness means to me. It can be a bit of a buzzword at times, but mindfulness is truly the art of being present. And being present can happen anytime. It doesn't always have to mean meditation or taking a yoga class, it can be simple daily tasks or actions. Like exercising and feeling the movements you are doing and being conscious of your body. Taking an intentionally deep breath and feeling your lungs expand. Taking a walk outside and noticing all that surrounds you; what the temperature feels like, sounds you hear, the colors in the trees. Eating meals with someone and having your phone away. Being truly present in a conversation. It is easy for my mind to wander just like anyone else, so I must constantly work on coming back to the present. As much as being present improves my mental and physical health, it also gives me a sense of gratitude. When I am present in a conversation, I feel a true sense of connection. When I am present on a hike or a walk, I am grateful for my life and experiences. When we allow our minds to wander to the future or back in the past, we miss all the moments that are happening right now.

Create Space: I create space by making boundaries in my life. This can include little changes such as not looking at my phone after work once I finish dinner. This allows me to decompress and allows my brain to not be overstimulated. Creating space has included big changes such as defining healthy and unhealthy relationships in my life. This can be tough because sometimes these relationships once were great but over time became toxic. I have learned how important it is to create boundaries in your life to make sure you have a healthy ecosystem that supports your wellness and doesn't take away from it.

Meditation: I would love to say that along with journaling and working on being present, I am the queen of meditation, but it just isn't true. I am still working on this one but I have found techniques that work for me such as physical relaxation, intentional and deep breathing, and guided meditations.

Physical Relaxation: My favorite and go-to meditative technique is body scanning. I do this by using the first minute to relax my entire body starting with the top of my head and moving all the way to my toes. I then use the next two minutes to focus only on my breath. This calms me down and centers me. It allows me to come back to the present moment, and with just being three minutes makes this a very attainable daily goal.

Guided Meditation: I also use two different apps for guided meditation: Calm and Headspace. Using these apps allows me to practice my meditation on my time and at my convenience.

Breathing Techniques: I use a few different breathing exercises to keep my mental health well and to train my nervous system. Trauma victims can have an overactive sympathetic nervous system stress response. This can cause you to have higher stress responses and can keep you in this state, which can have harmful effects on your health. I have worked on this by using a few different breathing exercises throughout the day that help me lower my anxiety and train my nervous system out of sympathetic and into parasympathetic (restful nervous system).

4-7-8 Breathing Technique: Breathe in for four seconds, hold your breath for seven seconds, and breathe out for eight seconds. Repeat five to eight times.

Foundation Training Decompression Technique: Decompression breathing realigns and opens your spine and diaphragm to bring in more oxygen to your brain and restores your nervous system. To do this, you can sit or stand and place your thumbs on the bottom of your ribcage and pinkies on your hip bones. Bring your chin back, close your eyes, breathe in, and try to lift your ribcage and head up to the ceiling creating length between your ribcage and hip bones. When you breathe out, don't lose the length. Repeat these two more times, lengthening your ribcage away from your hip bones. On the last breath, relax all the way.

Physical

Beyond the health benefits, exercise to me is my therapy. It reconnects my mind and body and on some days is the only time I get for myself. I look forward to going on a run or to the gym every day because it is my one hour for me. I get to clear my head and focus on my body. Since my attack, I have never taken this for granted because it took me a long time to love my body and get reacquainted with it. Working out in whatever fashion I choose makes me feel powerful. Feeling physically strong helps me feel mentally strong.

Get Moving: Just twenty minutes of physical exercise a day is proven to have many health benefits, such as lowering blood pressure, improving overall organ function and blood flow, and mental clarity. For me, I will carve out forty-five minutes a day for my workout. Sometimes that is hopping on my bike, going for a run, boxing, or going on a walk. I listen to my body and choose what I want to do based on how I am feeling that day. If I need to clear my head, I will go for a run or do some form of long-term cardio. If I am feeling down, I usually do weights or a strength workout because it makes me feel strong and accomplished.

Restore: Restore sessions are my favorite. These forty-five-minute sessions are just for foam rolling, breathing exercises, and stretching. High stress and anxiety gets stored in your body, so it is important to take time to reconnect and restore. Put on some relaxing music, dim the lights, spend some time releasing the tension stored in your muscles, and use this time to practice your breathing techniques.

Nutrition

Eat Healthy: I do not follow a diet because a diet to me is temporary. For me, nutrition is fuel, but most importantly, it's my medicine. It keeps me mentally well. Sugar, dairy, processed food, and grease all make me foggy and extremely anxious. These foods directly impact my mental health. All these foods have something in common; they all cause inflammation in the body. This inflammation causes disruptions in your nerve signals and causes your body to set off alarms. Being that 80 percent of our endorphins (happy hormones) come from the gut, it is no surprise that when your gut is inflamed, your mental clarity and mood may be impacted. Because of this, these foods can cause depression, anxiety, and chronic fatigue syndrome. I will be honest and tell you that I do not follow this 100 percent of the time, but I know the impact it has on my brain and body when I do eat these products, so I try to stick to my lifestyle most of the time.

Meal Prep: Meal prepping is very important for me. My days can be quite busy so if I do not pack my meals, sometimes I miss a meal. Meal prepping not only keeps me eating throughout the day, but also keeps me eating well. I try to meal prep on Sundays or Mondays after I grocery shop for the week.

Cut Back on Eating Out: Eating out not only costs a lot of money but you don't always know what is in your food when someone else is cooking it. Some restaurants can cook with oils, butter, sugar, and a ton of salt that disrupt your system and affect how you feel.

Make it Tasty: Most people think that eating healthy means it's tasteless and boring, but that is not true! There are so many resources out there now between cookbooks, YouTube, and Pinterest that give you easy, healthy recipes that you can make on your own. I get most of mine from Pinterest just by typing in "healthy lunches or dinners." This keeps me switching it up and making it interesting.

To summarize the steps above, wellness to me is about creating tools in your life that keep you well and help you become even better. My CliffsNotes would be to remember to breathe, get different perspectives, live for something greater than you, get to know others, take care of your body like it is your dream car, and grow to love and accept yourself. During your journey to wellness, remember to be kind and gentle to yourself. Meet yourself wherever you are and just take one step at a time. Progress happens from making daily baby steps. If you would like more resources, you can find Pancea in the Google and Apple app stores. We would love to have you a part of our community!

—**Ashley Hunt**, *CEO and founder of Pancea,*
and creator and cofounder of Nfinite Strength

CHAPTER 11

Being Dayna Whitmer

My parents are so lucky that I survived my leap from the Golden Gate. Over three thousand sets of parents have not been so blessed. Two of them are some of my dearest friends. What follows is the journey of the incredibly resilient, Dayna Whitmer and her late husband Mark, who along with their family and friends, tragically lost their son, Matthew to suicide from the Golden Gate Bridge, but I'll let her share her story of struggle and immense loss to advocacy and finding hope again.

Dayna Whitmer

I bolted upright in bed, wide awake from a sound sleep, and knew my world was forever changed. It sounds like an odd phrase, but it is exactly what happened to me the day my son, Matthew, disappeared.

It was a Thursday morning at 6:25 a.m. I woke and sat up suddenly. I couldn't describe what I was feeling, but my inner core knew something terrible had happened. My husband, Mark, was in the shower getting ready for work. I grabbed my robe to check on our sons, David and Matthew. Neither one was in his bed or room, so

I headed downstairs. The last time I saw the boys was the previous night when they were headed out for the evening, going to hang out with their friends.

Downstairs, David, twenty-two, was asleep on the couch. I woke him and asked him where Matthew was. He told me they had played video games until 1:30 a.m. and Matthew had gotten tired. He told David he wanted to sleep on the couch, but David wanted to continue with the video game. He said Matthew had been on the computer in the den for a while and then headed upstairs. He hadn't seen him since.

It wasn't unusual for Matt to go to a friend's house late at night when they got off work, and he often stayed at their place. From there he would head to classes at the National Holistic Institute, where he was training to become a massage therapist. He was four months away from graduating, and we had recently been discussing his plans for the future: working on a cruise ship or at an island spa.

Though he was twenty and very responsible, he knew I would worry in situations like this, so he would often leave a text message on my mobile phone. I checked it and had no text and no voice message either.

I tried calling his phone, my anxiety building. It rang four times and went to voicemail. I left him a message that I just was checking in with him and asked him to call me as soon as he could. I also left a text message in case he had his phone on vibrate or mute.

I went upstairs to get ready for work, a bit distracted and concerned. I tried several more times that morning to reach him. I had expressed my concerns to Mark and David, telling them that if they heard from Matthew to let me know. Work kept my mind occupied but there was a nagging sensation that something was still very wrong. I kept trying to reach Matt when he had a scheduled break at school and during his lunchtime.

I worked through lunch, sitting at my desk near the office phone with my mobile close by. At 1:15 p.m., I received a call from Mark.

My heart was pounding. He told me the Hercules Police had called him at work. Mark said it was something about Matthew's car in San Francisco. "He probably parked in the wrong place and got towed." He had been asked to contact the California Highway Patrol.

Matthew had been known to stay with friends in San Francisco but would misread the parking signs. He sometimes would get a ticket and he had been towed once before.

"No, no, no!" I cried into the phone, shaking my head, "It is worse than that. Find out and call me!"

Not two minutes later, Mark called back. He didn't even hesitate. "They think Matthew jumped off the Golden Gate Bridge this morning."

My heart stopped. I couldn't breathe. Mark had called the California Highway Patrol and received more information. They wanted to talk with us and have us pick up Matthew's car. Mark was going to meet me at home, and we would drive into the city together. Then one of us would need to drive Matt's car home.

I know at some time in our conversation, Mark told me Matt's car was in the parking lot by the bridge and a person was known to have jumped that morning based on eyewitnesses. I notified staff at work that I had an emergency and to cancel the rest of the patients scheduled in my clinic. I grabbed my purse and left. In the car, I started calling Matt's friends; had they heard from him? Any voice messages or texts? When was the last time they heard from him? Did they have the phone numbers of other people? It doesn't take more than fifteen minutes to get home, but I couldn't go fast enough.

When I walked in the door, David was sitting on the stairs, tears streaming down his face. "Is this real? Is Matthew really gone?"

Tears in my eyes, I hugged him and said, "It could be real. He might be gone; we don't know yet." I called a family friend to come stay with David—I did not want him to be alone. Sharon Jarrell called in to her work—she is an emergency room nurse—stating she had a family emergency, explained, and then headed over to the house. As we waited for Mark, we checked Matt's room for any letter or note that might indicate what happened. I didn't realize for weeks that a favorite stuffed animal of Matthew's, a sparkly chameleon, Quincy, was missing.

When Mark arrived, we thanked Sharon, hugged David, and headed out the door. We had to find out about this horrible mistake. This just couldn't be happening. But it could; in the back of our minds, we knew it was a distant possibly, but we just were not expecting this at all. Just two days earlier, Mark had received a shirt from his mother, Marione, for his birthday. It was the wrong size, but Matt liked the color. They agreed to exchange it for Matt's size.

Over the previous weekend, Matthew had talked with friends about what to do over the Thanksgiving weekend. He was making plans with them for gaming and just hanging out. During our drive to the Golden Gate Bridge, I received a call from a close friend, Judy. She lived next door with her husband, Pat, and son, Kyle. David and Matthew babysat Kyle for several years when he was very young.

We always joked that babysitting Kyle was a great form of birth control because our sons would come home from four or five hours of babysitting completely exhausted.

Judy said she had a call from Sharon about Matt and wanted to know specifically what was going on.

I told her what we knew: that someone jumped from the bridge, that Matthew's car was in the bridge parking lot and that we had not been able to reach him all day. She knew Matt's history of mental illness and expressed her concern and distress.

"Judy, I just don't know what we can tell Kyle," I said.

"That's okay," she said, "I have you on speakerphone and Kyle is in the car with me. He is listening to everything we are saying."

I had no words. My heart broke for Kyle: his first experience with death, and it was a dear friend. I told Judy I would call her when we knew more.

When we reached the parking lot, we found Matthew's car and there was a yellow tag on it with the markings "10-99," which indicates a possible suicide, but we didn't know that then. The highway patrol officer saw us and came over to talk to us. He gave us a few more specifics about what happened that morning. There were two women jogging and as they came around the south tower to the midspan of the bridge, they said they saw a young man look up at them and then quickly flung himself over the railing; he vaulted over the railing. It was a split-second decision. One woman looked to see where his body landed in the water, and the other called 911 to report the jump. Within five minutes, the U.S. Coast Guard was in the water below the bridge, actively searching for Matthew.

They searched for him for over ninety minutes but were unsuccessful. The CHP officer did explain that it can take a long time for body recovery and that there are some cases when the bodies are never recovered.

I know we were so much in shock we weren't quite sure what to do. Mark asked the officer to show him where Matthew jumped. The officer agreed and we made a very long walk out to light standard ninety-seven. Mark leaned against the rail and looked over and just started crying. He could not believe his son had done this; could not believe that he was forever gone. After a while, when Mark was ready, we returned to the cars. The officers asked if they could check Matthew's car just to check if there was any information that might help them in their investigation.

We saw the scatter of papers on his back seat, where his résumé provided the officers with information other than the registration, which was Mark's. Oddly enough, in the trunk, there was a full set of clothing still sopping wet. The clothes had the odor of ocean and oil, and we knew there was a recent incidence of an oil tanker striking the San Francisco–Oakland Bay Bridge in the previous week. The four of us looked at each other and I asked, "Has anyone seen a naked man walking around?" We had no idea what this was about. Did Matt jump, survive, come back to his car, and then just wander off due to the trauma of the jump? How did no one notice? Had he jumped the bridge, survived, and today returned to complete his mission?

After some discussion with the officers about what the next steps would be (filing the missing person's report, waiting for body recovery) we were ready to leave. I knew there was no way Mark would be able to drive Matthew's car. I got in his car, pulling the extra keys out of my purse. On the seat was his wallet with his ID, credit card, pictures, and CDs on the floor. When I started the car, the stereo came on. The last song he was listening to was from a Death Cab for Cutie CD. I remembered how Matt loved their *Transatlanticism* CD—how unique their music was. I was too much in shock to realize what song was playing when the engine turned on, so I don't know the specific last song he heard before he died.

We took the fastest way home, which meant going over the Golden Gate Bridge. I didn't focus on the bridge, much less the walkway, but I did look at light standard ninety-seven, not sure what I expected to see. I needed to get home. I just remember speaking out loud in the car, repeatedly telling or yelling at Matthew to call me or give me some sort of sign, so I knew where he was or what happened to him.

When we arrived home, I recall Sharon and David telling us they searched the house looking for a note or anything on the computer that might indicate what he did or why he did it. They did find that Matt had searched the Golden Gate Bridge website about the suicide deterrent, and it showed it was not in place but still just being considered.

I remember talking with Matt about this, the lack of suicide barriers, after he saw the movie *The Bridge*, which was released in 2006. We talked about how incredibly senseless it was to not have a barrier in place when this bridge was a "weapon of mass destruction," as he so aptly put it, being too available to suicidal people.

Later that evening, Mark called the crisis line number the CHP officer had given us, and he spoke with a crisis counselor. They did offer eight weeks of crisis counseling in groups that they had only recently started, so it would be another six weeks before Mark or I could get into the groups. Mark spoke with the counselor for almost an hour that evening.

Geeta, our neighbor who was home when the Hercules Police came by our house and provided them with Mark's contact information, came by that evening. She was so concerned about what happened and how we were dealing with this. Geeta came over every evening for over a month to check on us and bring us food. We were close over the years, sharing time with her young daughters and having a few "tea parties" with hats and feather boas.

That evening, I didn't know what to do, but I had to do something, so I started calling all hospitals in the area, the ones in San Francisco and Marin County. I asked for Matthew by name, and I asked for a John Doe. The problem was the new HIPAA or privacy laws, so the staff could not tell me specifically if Matt was in the emergency room or not. I explained the situation and asked them to at least call the police if there was somebody fitting Matt's description and type of trauma. I think it was more awkward for the staff on the other end of the line than it was for me. Other friends called to express concern, their love, and to see if there was any news. We told them it was a wait-and-see situation.

Mark called our cell phone company to see if they could help locate Matthew's phone. It was so frustrating; even though it was our property, we were told we had to get a subpoena to obtain access to their records since Matthew was an adult and not classified as a missing person as of yet. We knew when we called Matt that morning that the phone would take four rings before going to voicemail. This evening, we noticed it went directly to voicemail. The following day, the CHP was able to contact the cell phone company. They were able to determine there was a final ping off a local tower by the Golden Gate Bridge.

I couldn't sleep for several nights. Maybe a few minutes here and there, but I would lie down with the landline and cell phone on my chest. Scenarios just kept playing through my mind of what had happened over the previous date or week. What really happened? Did Matt jump or was that another mother's son? Did Matt leave with another person or leave the area on his own? Was there anything I missed? Anything I did wrong? Where was Matthew? Why hadn't he used his cell phone, credit card, or ATM card?

The next day—the next day we had to start dealing with the reality of this, the reality of telling our families of our loss, that *perhaps* Mattie was gone. I started the calls. I knew my mom in Oregon went to the gym with my oldest sister, Debbie, every morning around 7 a.m. I hadn't slept so I called my older sister, Dianne, in Wisconsin, around 5 a.m. She was two hours ahead, and I knew she wakes early.

How do you tell someone something like this, so early in the day? Such a blunt, brutal fact? It started with, "I don't know how to say this so let me just say what I know." I told her how I was told, and she would not believe it. She didn't want to believe it any more than I did.

Dianne is the one I turned to in need, and I needed her guidance on how to deliver this news to our mother. Her idea was to call Debbie, tell her the situation, and when she arrived at Mom's house, Debbie would call me on her cell, and then hand the phone to Mom so I could tell her.

I called Debbie shortly after, must have been 6 a.m., when she normally gets up. I explained the situation and apologized in putting her in this position, having to be with Mom at a time like this.

Like clockwork, it happened, and my mother was devastated. I could never express to Debbie what it meant to have her there for me. Mom wanted to come down to us immediately, but we asked her to wait. We were hoping to have some news of recovery. She didn't care about that but waited for us, as we asked.

Before the day was over, Dianne called and told me that as she was on her knees, scrubbing her kitchen floors (her therapy), she decided she and her daughter, Tracy, a physician in Chicago, would come to us and had already made travel arrangements. I believe their motive was more than just Matthew.

Dianne was my confidante when I was first diagnosed with depression, the only family member who originally knew of my psychosis and hospitalizations due to suicidal ideation or attempts.

After Dianne and Tracy arrived, they talked with me about the issues with Matthew. Dianne said, "I don't understand, you and Matthew had such an open relationship, you shared everything."

It was then that I told them what we learned over the past few days. Matthew had tried to contact friends to talk with; on the Monday night before his disappearance, he had called friends, had spoken of his desperation. That was the same night that he came home late and went into the hot tub outside. He called David on his cell phone (in the house) to bring him a towel. David said Matt didn't have any clothes outside with him.

We think that explains the wet clothes in his trunk; we think he made a suicide attempt on Monday night. Later in the night, Matt came into our bathroom, vomiting. The boys' bathroom was under construction and a toilet was not available.

I woke and asked him if he was all right. Now, years later, I see him in the doorway, and I can only recall him saying, "Yes." but I question my memory. Was I really cognizant of his response? Now when I wake late at night, I wonder if I heard what he really said versus what I heard. I am scared that I missed him saying that he was *not* okay and needed help, but I fell back to sleep, so maybe he felt that I no longer cared. Did I cause his death because of that?

After an initial night of no sleep, we decided to touch base with others involved in Matt's life. We started with the school Matthew was attending for massage therapy and decided to meet with the director. When we got there, she was very upset about the news concerning Matt but understanding and helpful considering the circumstances. She explained to us that Matthew had not been in class since the previous Wednesday, eight days prior. This was quite a surprise, especially for me.

Every morning, Matt and I would have conversations while he was getting ready for school. He was self-conscious about his looks and his blemishes so I would help cover them up with facial foundation before he left for the day. Our conversations dealt with work, school, people with attitudes, and his health. We had done this every school day for that week, and I was none the wiser. It would only be later that I discovered Matt was hearing voices again.

Matthew's History

The possibility of Matthew jumping from the bridge was real.

Matt was twelve when on the first day of school for eighth grade, he wouldn't get out of bed. He said he didn't feel well. When I pressed him, he told me he tried to hang himself with his belt the night before but it wouldn't stay tight. He eventually got tired and fell asleep.

I asked him if he still felt suicidal and he said yes. I told him to rest, and I went downstairs. I called the pediatrician and waited for the answering service to patch me through. I explained the situation to the doctor, and he advised me to take him to the emergency room. He would call ahead.

I went back upstairs and explained to Matt what we needed to do. He would nod or say, "Okay." It was clear from his expression and responses he was mostly void of emotion. Or his pain was so great he had to cover himself in a shell for emotional protection. I knew this too well given my own history.

He followed directions and was able to dress himself and went willingly to the car. We drove to the hospital and arrived at the emergency room. Here he was interviewed, had his blood drawn, and a urine sample taken. Then we waited. Staff determined he was a threat to himself and continued to interview him.

We waited for confirmation there was a bed available at the mental health campus of the hospital and we were able to drive him there. Our family knew the building and procedures well because of my hospitalizations.

Matthew was admitted and that was when things changed. Because of the policies around mental health and privacy issues, Mark and I had limited opportunity or input in Matt's care.

After several days of evaluations, Mark and I were interviewed by the staff, which included psychiatric RNs and licensed clinical social workers (LCSWs).

They reviewed packets of questionnaires they had Matt's teacher and us complete and they asked Mark and me questions. After an hour of interaction, the part that dumbfounded Mark and I was when they told us that Matthew was bored; he didn't have enough stimulation.

Mark and I looked at each other and looked back at them across the table.

"Bored? How could Matthew be bored? Do you know what he did this summer? He learned how to play drums, speak Japanese, eat sushi, draw cartoons, be active in Boy Scouts, spend a week at camp, play with friends, have LAN (Local Access Network) parties, and go to Marine World several times. He swam every day, played bingo and cards, learned to cook, and rode his bike. How is that boring?"

It was their turn to look surprised.

From what we gathered, Matthew had been having problems throughout the summer. Matthew told the staff the voices had started after he smoked marijuana with a friend. He began hearing the Devil telling him to kill himself. I later learned that marijuana, especially if laced with another substance, could be a trigger for schizophrenia or psychotic episodes. Matthew was placed on medication because he was hearing voices and for his depression.

These medications can make the brain chemistry unstable until they reach their therapeutic levels. Medications made for adults will have different effects on children and young adults. Their brains keep growing until they are twenty-five. Here was Mattie at twelve. It is hard to imagine what his thoughts would have been, even more frightening because of what these medications were doing to his brain.

On the third day, I received a call from a nurse manager at the hospital. It was about 11 a.m. and she told me Matthew was being taken to the emergency room. He had been able to tie a pillowcase tightly around his neck, cutting off his air supply. He lost consciousness.

One of the other patients alerted the nursing staff. They took prompt action but were unable to untie the pillowcase. They needed to use scissors to cut through the fabric and had scraped his skin. He was all right but taken to the hospital for X-rays to ensure he had not damaged his hyoid bone, which could compromise his airway. Fortunately, he had not. Even though this was a traumatic event, we were *not* allowed to see him until visiting hours that evening.

Matthew was diagnosed with schizoaffective disorder with psychotic features. Schizoaffective disorder is a mental disorder characterized by a disordered thought process (psychosis) with a mood disorder.

Common symptoms of psychosis include auditory hallucinations, paranoid delusions, and disorganized speech and thinking. Schizoaffective disorder is divided into two mood disorder types: bipolar or depressive. The bipolar type is distinguished by symptoms of mania, hypomania, or mixed episodes; the depressive type by symptoms of depression exclusively. The onset of symptoms usually begins in young adulthood. It would be clear that Matthew had the bipolar type due to the periods of mania he experienced.

It would take a few weeks before Matthew was able to come home. And we knew that it takes time for psychiatric medications to take effect. He wasn't home a week when he told me that he did not feel safe any longer, so we immediately went back to the hospital. It would take another few weeks before he was able to come home, but then what?

Our family was in shock when we heard the diagnosis and scrambled for information. One of the best organizations for families like ours is the National Alliance on Mental Illness (NAMI). They are a grassroots organization that educates and teaches consumers with mental illnesses and their families to advocate to ensure they have access to mental health care and housing and ensure treatment at the time it is needed.

This organization helped us understand the disorder Matthew had, how to handle it, and how to secure the best care possible. This included finding a child psychiatrist. There were few in the Bay Area and it was difficult to find one accepting new patients. We had no idea there were so many children needing treatment!!

For Matthew, his treatment consisted of medications and therapies. Yet he still needed to be prepared for life, and that included school.

School

School was a challenge. As soon as we knew that Matthew's issue was going to be a chronic lifelong medical issue, we went to the school. He was in eighth grade, so he had five years to complete, if possible. We met with his teacher and the school psychologist. They had us complete many forms. We had forms to take to Matthew and his doctors at the hospital, essentially to anyone who was involved with his care. The staff at Carquinez Middle School and the entire John Swett school district were the greatest. We did an urgent evaluation and were able to place Matthew in special education for emotionally disturbed students.

He was put on an individual education plan (IEP) for those with emotional disorders. Initially, he couldn't come home on a full-time basis. They have something called a partial hospitalization program where students like Matthew stay at the hospital as an outpatient for several hours each day. They get some school structure and then come home.

This went on for several weeks and during this time I had to take time off from work. Mark was traveling with his work, often to other countries, but I had incredibly understanding supervisors who allowed me to take the time off I needed. I had to permanently cut back my position from full time to three-quarter time to care for Matt.

Being part-time allowed me to take Matthew to the partial hospital program in the morning then pick him up in the afternoon and stay with him the remainder of the time. When he was feeling better, we met with staff at his school in the John Swett school district to determine if he could remain in a classroom setting or if we needed to look at alternatives.

One day, the psychologists at the school district called and said they had an incredible opportunity for Matthew. The Contra Costa County mental health program has a school called the Floyd I. Marchus Counseling and Education Program, or the Marchus School. It is a special education school for emotionally disturbed students. It rotates the openings to different districts and different schools. It is very difficult to get into the school. To be fair to all the different districts and schools in the county, when they have an opening, they have to offer that opening to the next district. We were lucky our district was next on the list and Matthew's grade was where they had the opening!

Our family talked it over with Matthew, and he was agreeable to doing this. We made arrangements for me to take him there and pick him up every day, which required changes in my work schedule again.

Matthew spent several months at the Marchus School and then was transferred on certain days to the local junior high school to adjust into mainstream school. While he was at the junior high school, he became part of the "Peer-to-Peer" program, which is students helping students in need, offering kids someone to talk to, someone who cares, someone who has "been there."

He enjoyed his time there and made connections with teachers and other students. It was a little frustrating at times having to deal with other students more ill than him. Matthew improved quickly in personal approaches and his scores were very good. His disorder was under control so the school staff, with our agreement, transitioned Matt into a regular school. Matt started with several days per week and then eventually full-time school at Martinez Junior High School for the last three months of the school year. He graduated from Marchus School at the end of the school year, and he was ready to go back to the John Swett school district.

After summer, he started at John Swett High School in the ninth grade now, but he had a difficult time with the "maturity" level of the other students. After a quick discussion with the IEP team, Matthew was settled into homeschool, where the district would send a teacher to the house twice a week. This was more intensive, but Matthew was able to adapt. He became more organized and more challenged.

Before he entered the tenth grade, he passed the California High School Exit Exam. This is a requirement to graduate in our state. He also passed the California High School Equivalency Exam at the same time. The equivalency exam gave him a high school diploma and he could have left school immediately. However, when he was informed that he would not get all the high school credits he needed to move on to college, he opted to stay in school and added college courses in the evening at the local community college. At this time, Matthew was nominated for People to People by one of his teachers. P2P is a student ambassador program in which young adults like Matthew travel to other countries, learn about the people and their culture, and represent The US and its culture. He was stable both in school and his illness. Matt was interested in this trip and very confident in himself, so we attended the conferences and made the arrangements.

In July 2004, Mattie traveled for three weeks with People to People to England, Wales, and Ireland. The trip also included two home stays, during which the students stay at people's homes for a more in-depth cultural exchange. One of his best experiences was staying at a farm in Ireland and being woken in the morning by a cow mooing in his window. He said he was amazed by the many shades of green that covered Ireland. He very much wanted to return and discover more about his heritage.

He came home an independent and confident man at the age of sixteen and ready to take on the world. It was hard to see any of the symptoms of his disorder.

Matthew was able to attend his senior year in the classroom and graduated with his class in 2005. He worked and attended some college classes after graduation but when he was nineteen, he decided he wanted to learn massage therapy. He felt this would allow him to help other people heal and that this was somewhat an art form.

Without recovery of Matthew's body, we remained in a limbo state, likely still in shock. We did not know what to do but we needed to take some sort of action. Within a few weeks after Matthew's disappearance, David asked us if we had any plans for a service or vigil for Matthew. Students in his class were wondering so we planned for a candlelight vigil at Port Isabel in Richmond. It is in the East Bay with a full view of the Golden Gate Bridge.

People arrived shortly before sunset and we lit candles, talked about Matthew, and shared memories and poems, while the sun was setting beyond the bridge and Mount Tamalpias. As the vigil was ending, a friend tapped me on the shoulder and pointed towards Mount Tam. The observatory at the top of the mountain was opening and its light was shining directly into the heavens. We all stopped and paused for a moment, feeling Matthew was showing us just where he was, watching us, from the heavens above. A short time later, after the first of the year, I found an advertisement for the National Alliance on Mental Illness (NAMI) walk (NAMIWalk) in the Bay Area. All nine county chapters were having a walk to raise funds to keep their free education programs going.

NAMI

NAMI is a grassroots organization that has grown over the years since 1979, helping families like ours learn how to deal with mental health issues. NAMI offers education programs to hundreds of families, individuals, and educators to get the support and information they need. NAMI shapes the national public policy landscape for people with mental illness and their families. Public awareness events and activities, including NAMIWalks, successfully combat stigma and encourage understanding. When Matthew was diagnosed with schizoaffective disorder, we had no clue what that meant much less how we were supposed to deal with it. NAMI provided the information on the disorder, what to expect, how to advocate for Matthew, and how to take care of us.

Mark, David, and I talked about joining the NAMIWalk in our area and decided we would do this. We would be "Mattie's Boondock Saints" with a slogan of "For suicides to continue, let good people do nothing." Friends and family were excited to do something for Matthew. Our first walk was in May 2008, just over six months after he went missing. We walked the Bay Area San Francisco NAMIWalk for eight years. Each year, we saw it grow larger and larger with more walkers and speakers such as Patty Duke, Kevin Hines—a survivor from a bridge jump—and Kevin Briggs, a retired CHP officer who saved over two hundred people by talking them back over the railing. I was honored to speak at the NAMIWalk kickoff luncheon in 2011. We are proud that we raised funds for Contra Costa NAMI while helping raise awareness about mental health issues. We also do what we can on a state level when advocating to the legislature for action.

AFSP

Another mother who lost her son at the bridge was a member of the American Foundation for Suicide Prevention. She had encouraged me to join their outreach program, which provided volunteers to meet with newly bereaved families, at their request, to let them know they're not alone in their situation of suicide loss and to provide resources for them. I did this and have been out on several visits. It is a good feeling to know I'm helping people understand suicide and provide support, the same as I received. I also signed up to be a field advocate when needed for legislative issues, such as when the Mental Health Parity Act came up, and do what I can locally.

BridgeRail Foundation

In my quest to find answers and get clarity, I made an appointment to visit the Marin County coroner, Ken Holmes, who was responsible for the victims of Golden Gate Bridge suicides. Mr. Holmes spoke with me for over an hour. He answered my questions and concerns about going to look for Matthew's body. I felt guilty for not hiring a boat to try and search for him. Ken assured me that it was probably a good thing I didn't. It would be a waste of time and money because I wouldn't know how to search.

Mr. Holmes explained that the United States Coast Guard (USCG) has training in doing this because the bodies don't always come back up to the surface. He explained that when the bodies hit the water, there is massive internal damage and many bones are broken. If the person doesn't die on impact, they are often unconscious and drown without gaining consciousness. He said the body would sometimes float with the limbs dangling down and only the back facing the surface. The body would appear more as a small square or rectangular shape in the water. Of course, the color of the clothing they wore would make a difference.

He did agree with Mark and I that if Matt's body had washed up on the shores somewhere locally, it would have been reported. We had hoped with all the oil in the water and all the people combing the shores to protect animals and birds, we would have had a greater chance at recovery.

Ken and I talked about the lack of information and guidance given to families like ours. We were told that the highway patrol was going to submit a missing person's report. That was not the case. A missing person's report needed to be filed in the city of residence for the person.

Mr. Holmes did tell me that it could take up to six months for body recovery. He encouraged me to call any medical examiner's or coroner's office within the Bay Area and up and down the coast. This became a monthly routine. I would place my calls and ask if there was a body or remains that could be those of a young male who had gone missing in mid-November. I would often be asked the circumstances of his disappearance and I would explain that we thought he jumped off the Golden Gate Bridge, so he would have been found near the coast with extensive long-term water damage to his body. Everyone I spoke with every month over a six-month period was incredibly compassionate and very understanding. They understood how difficult it was for me to make those calls to try to find my son.

Around this time, while searching the internet, I came across the website for BridgeRail Foundation. I emailed them and asked if they could help me. I needed to know if it was unusual for somebody to go missing for such a long time. I was surprised to receive a response within twenty-four hours. It was from David Hull, president of BridgeRail Foundation (BRF). He told me about his daughter Kathy, who died by jumping off the bridge. He also asked me if I wanted to talk with others in this situation.

I agreed and within moments, I received a call from another mother who lost her son Matthew at the bridge—Matty, as she called him. His body was missing for six days and was found miles south along the coast from San Francisco.

I received other calls and felt a sense of, well, not exactly relief, but knowing I wasn't alone in all of this. Someone else understood the pain and frustration of a missing loved one.

Dave Hull also told me the best action I could take was to talk to the board of directors of the Golden Gate Bridge district. They met on Fridays once a month at the offices at the bridge toll plaza.

Dave also had meetings with the families of the suicide victims, survivors of suicide loss, through the BridgeRail Foundation. We met irregularly but it was so important to be around others who not only lost a loved one, but lost them to this bridge, with and without body recovery.

These meetings were during our extreme grief, shock, and post-traumatic stress situations, yet many families coalesced. Our family suffered a loss in November of 2007, another family in December 2007, the Brookses in January 2008, and the Barkses in February 2008. The timing and the families were unique and because we became so entwined, we were able to strongly support each other and allow ourselves to take our loss and grief to the public. Through volunteering for BridgeRail Foundation, we were able to direct our energies for a purpose, and that purpose was stopping suicides from the Golden Gate Bridge.

Matthew and I would have lively talks about politics, and I always encouraged him to vote, though he felt it would be useless. I always told him it only takes one person to make a difference. Now I needed to follow through on that advice. I had never done public speaking in my life. It was part of the reason I stopped taking college courses, because I was flunking out of my public speaking class.

So, I started speaking at the GGB district board of directors' meetings. I always started by identifying myself as the mother of Matthew, who has been missing since November 15, 2007. I spoke of the newly established California Office of Suicide Prevention with the motto, "Every Californian is part of the solution." I spoke about the Americans with Disabilities Act and asked them to consider those with mental health disabilities who came to their structure, which was a hazard to their health. I requested the BOD to consider closing the walkway until a barrier was in place.

I was coming somewhat late to these endeavors. There had been so many others struggling for decades to stop these suicides. The GGB district had wind-tunnel studies done in 2005 to determine what deterrent/barrier could be put onto the bridge without compromising its structural integrity. In July 2008, there were two public hearings, one held in San Francisco and the other in Marin County, that demonstrated the five options to build a barrier or not to build anything. People were also allowed to request information online or through the mail. The GGB district also had an open public comment period where people could address their opinions about these barriers.

Through resources at work, I was able to gather twenty-two abstracts from scientific journals with peer-reviewed articles about the effectiveness of suicide prevention by restricting access to lethal means. At the August 2008 meeting, Mark, my husband, spoke to the GGB district BOD about these abstracts and provided copies to each member. Reading the minutes of the meeting several weeks later, we were surprised to read that the board members asked staff to obtain the complete articles, all twenty-two, so they could be better versed on the subject.

This meant change! For the first time, the board members were willing to learn and understand the causes and prevention methods for suicide. This is so incredibly important because, soon, the time would come for them to vote for a deterrent or not, and if yes, what option. When they voted, they would be doing it with knowledge and understanding of the subject.

After a review of the public input and based on reports and evaluations from the GGB district engineering department, the board of directors voted on October 10, 2008, with a vote of fifteen ayes and one no, to select Alternative 3—the net—as the Locally Preferred Alternative (LPA).

Now the only problem was to get the funding. In November, the BRF held a conference with workshops to gather people who would help organize the mental health community, be advocates to talk with Congress, and act as the administration for the funding for the net. The bridge district did not have any of this money available.

BRF knew the millions of dollars for the project would primarily be funded by the federal government. In 2009, BRF members and family volunteers joined ranks and started visiting all the congressional senators and representatives in the Bay Area in all the counties. The idea was to modify the wording of the transportation bill to be more inclusive of safety features on roadways and bridges. After several months went by, there was a letter to Congress and signed by nearly every Bay Area representative, including Senators Barbara Boxer and Dianne Feinstein, stating they were in support of a change in the transportation bill to include funding available for suicide barriers as a public safety issue.

Unfortunately, the bill was not renewed; it was simply extended so no changes were made. This would cause a delay of eighteen to twenty-four months. During that time, BRF worked with mental health community partners such as NAMI and AFSP to garner national support for the change when the transportation bill came up for renewal again.

Funding was found during this time to initiate the environmental impact report, and the bridge district proceeded with that. The district BOD certified the "Final Environmental Impact Report Released for Golden Gate Bridge Physical Suicide Deterrent System Project" on February 12, 2010.

In 2009, at the AFSP Out of the Darkness walk held at Crissy Field in San Francisco, BRF members, families, and other volunteers gathered sixteen hundred pairs of shoes, the estimated number of victims of GGB suicide, and laid them out in full view of the bridge. Many families brought actual shoes their loved ones had worn for the display. This was called the "Whose Shoes?" Visual Memorial, so people could see and appreciate the number of lives lost at this site. It was a powerful display and garnered local press with photos and interviews of families, including myself.

The "Whose Shoes?" was put on display at various sites over the years, though sometimes it was just a tabletop display with just a few shoes and information about the BridgeRail Foundation. At each display, we started gathering signatures for the petition to ask the bridge district to select a deterrent option. We gathered more than four hundred in a short time and included many comments from people around the world who signed the online petition. This was submitted to the district BOD to encourage them to keep working on this issue.

In 2010, I represented BRF to help coordinate the Please Don't Jump Day in San Francisco, the next "Whose Shoes?" display was in association with the Pick Up the Phone tour with the Kristin Brooks Hope Center/National Hopeline Network. This was in conjunction with the PostSecret postcard that said, "I have lived in San Francisco since I was young. I am illegal. I am not wanted here. I don't belong anywhere. This summer I plan to jump off the Golden Gate."

A woman in Canada started a Facebook page and out of that grew into the Please Don't Jump Day in San Francisco in 2010. This was an awareness event held on September 22, 2010, again, in San Francisco at Crissy Field, in full view of the Golden Gate Bridge. Participants were encouraging people to learn warning signs of a potential suicide and asking them not to jump if they were in crisis. The music group Blue October headlined it with speakers Tom Ammiano (a member of the state assembly), Kevin Hines, myself representing BridgeRail Foundation, and other suicide prevention advocates. Right next to the bandstand was "Whose Shoes?" again causing much reflection of the number of lives lost.

The event was covered by ABC, NBC, CBS, and FOX News as Tom Ammiano presented a proclamation declaring September 22 "Please Don't Jump Day." What I remember most of that event was a young woman who told me how sorry she was that I lost my son and that what I said made her realize that she never wanted her mother to feel the way I did, despite her mental illness and suicidal tendencies. She promised to be more attentive to her own care. We cried and hugged each other.

Over the years of the progress of a barrier there were newspaper articles about the bridge, suicides, and barriers, including the cost, so incredibly high at $45 million at that time. After reading the articles, I would venture into the comment sections. It's difficult to read comments like "It cleans the gene pool," "They'll just go somewhere else," "Let's put in a diving board," and "Let's charge for them to jump."

It's hard reading that as a parent. It hurts each time I read those statements. My son, Matthew, was ill. Trying to alleviate pain when there's no medication and no therapy that can remove it quickly enough, most people would attempt suicide, often within the hour of the thought. People who don't sleep well and have mental illness often come to these crossroads with suicidal ideation. Matthew had not been sleeping well. But he also covered up what was going on by telling different people different things, assuring me he was fine, putting on a façade that he was happy. I'm guilty because I let my guard down when he had a mental disorder. I let my guard down and I pay for that every day.

If only Matt had gone somewhere else and tried another method of suicide, he would likely be here today. The issue with suicide methods is lethality and a Golden Gate Bridge jump is over 98 percent lethal. The reason why overdosing or poisons aren't as effective is because people have time to think about what they just did. They have time to make a call and correct their actions.

It's less than four seconds from jumping off the bridge to hitting the water. I know it was impulsive for Matthew from the comments of the witnesses and I believe there was instant regret as soon as he bolted over the railing. What woke me up that morning was his final call for help to me.

These victims have a brain illness that manifests as a mental disease or disorder and the crisis of this mental illness is suicide ideation, attempt, and completion. How can anyone think that is a choice? That a person can snap out of depression? Think hallucinating is a choice?

Suicide is not unlike diabetes or heart disease when it becomes a crisis. Do we fault the person who makes the choice to not take their insulin then causes a car accident and kills people? The person with heart disease who doesn't take his medication and has a heart attack, do we not give him CPR because he made a choice? Of course not! The same holds true for the person with a brain disease especially when they aren't able to think well. They feel they have no other choice to end their pain.

Often, I took the bait in the newspaper comments and responded, trying to enlighten people about facts and not old myths. One woman kept responding to me, trying to disprove my statements.

I finally asked her if she had children. Yes, she had a teenage daughter. "So, are you willing to risk her life, thinking she feels down or depressed because of PMS and not for a mental health issue? Are you willing to wake up one morning and find she is gone forever because you don't want to verify the facts I am posting?"

After a lengthy pause, she responded, asking me for a website about teenagers and depression. I gave her seven sites and thanked her for being open-minded. I am grateful because there were so many others posting comments who saw our exchange and I hope a few took my comments to heart.

Many families, survivors of suicide loss, did the same, responding to the online comments, working to educate and inform people. There were other families who shared their stories with the public through letters to editors of local papers, doing local television and news interviews, and even sharing their story on national television.

Because of all the arguments raised about the amount of money required to build the net and the belief that the suicide rate would not change if these people attempted with another method of suicide, I started looking at documentation I had collected over the years. After some discussion with my supervisor, Dr. David Woods, we decided to write a paper to address these issues. "Analysis of the Cost Effectiveness of a Suicide Barrier on the Golden Gate Bridge," which reviewed data of suicides in San Francisco and the Golden Gate Bridge over seven decades. It reviewed the frequency of a method compared with its lethality against the Value of a Statistical Life (VSL).

The US Department of Transportation (United States Department of Transportation, 2009) estimates the value of a life saved to be worth $3.2 to $8 million, based on regional factors including average income. The GGB connects two of the wealthiest counties in

California, San Francisco County and Marin County, with median family incomes that are respectively 39.8 percent and 72 percent above the national average. Therefore, the appropriate statistical value of life would be at the high end of the USDOT range. Assuming that the twenty-year cost of the GGB suicide barrier is $51.6 million, and that it results in the saving of 286 lives, the cost per life saved is $180,419, well under 6 percent of the minimal USDOT VSL. This suggests that the GGB suicide barrier would be a highly cost-effective highway safety project.

The paper was published in a peer-reviewed journal, *Crisis*, the journal for the International Association of Suicide Prevention, in January 2013. The conclusion says it all:

> *The GGB remains one of the most lethal suicide sites in the world lacking a suicide barrier. With nonphysical interventions proven to be only moderately effective, a physical barrier remains the only preventative system that will completely stop GGB suicides. We evaluated the cost-effectiveness of a proposed barrier using the conservative assumptions that (1) all GGB suicides would attempt suicide with alternate methods, (2) all GGB suicides were witnessed or verified by autopsy, and (3) survivors of attempted suicide using alternative methods would eventually commit suicide at high rates (12–13%). Our results suggest that the proposed GGB suicide barrier would save lives in a highly cost-effective manner because of the reduced lethality of alternate suicide methods in comparison with jumps from the GGB.*

I took the findings and presented them to the Golden Gate Bridge District BOD in February 2013 to emphasize that lethality of a suicide method is critical and the methods with the highest lethality need the quickest resolution. Despite the cost of the net being so high, this was still cost-effective when looking at the cost of a life.

BRF heard the news that the bridge district was planning the seventy-fifth anniversary of the opening of the bridge. They were organizing groups to help commemorate the events and one of them was a community partner for the festival. I had heard from many families that they did not want the suicides ignored at this festival; they did not want their children's lives to be overlooked.

The BridgeRail Foundation submitted for and was accepted as one of the seventy-five community partners for their festival. This was the most important "Whose Shoes?" display. We used chalk mark outlines of shoes to recognize those suspected but missing victims like my son, Matthew. To be acknowledged by not only the bridge district, but the other coordinators of this event including the Golden Gate National Parks Conservancy, the National Park Service, Golden Gate National Parks, the Presidio Trust, and the city and county of San Francisco was affirming for our foundation and every family, every person who is a survivor of suicide loss at this site.

Our family wasn't there that day to volunteer for the BRF, to set up the display and talk to the people walking by. Over a year before we had planned to have a memorial for Matthew. Mark, David, and I decided it would be best to have it on the weekend of his birthday, Memorial Day weekend. Matthew's birthday falls on May 28. We invited friends and family from near and far to attend that weekend. We ordered white roses from Ecuador and soil from Ireland to make up bouquets for Matthew. We chartered a bus to take everyone out to the bridge to say a final farewell and lay flowers on Matthew's gravesite, just under light standard ninety-seven.

The bridge district was considerate and helped us make these arrangements for our event. The parking lots were closed because of the seventy-fifth anniversary festival but the bridge district permitted us to park our charter bus to bring our family and friends to Matthew's gravesite, light standard ninety-seven.

As we all left the bus, we handed everyone a bouquet of roses with bags of Irish soil attached. Of course, we used biodegradable bags and paper twine since these would be tossed into the waters of the bay. We were grateful there weren't many pedestrians on the bridge. Several of us encountered people that were curious about the groups carrying the multitude of roses.

I was walking a short way with Gloria, the woman who lost her son, Matty, when a gentleman with a question approached us. He said, "I know the bridge has an anniversary but why are so many people carrying roses?"

Gloria responded, "The roses are for a memorial for her son that she lost from the bridge." His response was, "I'm sorry. I have lived in San Francisco all my life, and I know the bridge district has done a lot to stop the suicides, but not enough."

Gloria said, "Thank you, we have both lost our sons, our Matthews, on this bridge."

I must mention this wonderful woman had never been on the bridge in her life and for the love of our sons, she walked past the south tower to light standard ninety-seven to toss a bouquet for her son. She doesn't know where her Matty jumped. Gloria couldn't remain and returned to help with the shuttle of volunteers for the BridgeRail Foundation "Whose Shoes?" Visual Memorial.

I think the most special thing about Matthew's memorial was a few days before everyone came into town, a pigeon flew into our yard and decided to stay. It was a homing pigeon with a band on its leg. This pigeon stayed while we had barbecues that weekend. It wandered around on the ground, fearless of people sitting and visiting. It happily ate birdseed and drank water placed under the tables. It stayed a few more days after everyone went home and then flew away.

I looked up online to see what a pigeon represents and as a totem sign it represents home, the desire to come home, to be at home, be surrounded by loved ones. I firmly believe that Matthew was that pigeon, and he knew we were all here to celebrate his life.

In 2013, the BridgeRail Foundation and the families assisted Assembly member Tom Ammiano on his bill AB 755, which would provide that during construction or reconstruction of a bridge in California, the need for a suicide barrier must be considered.

Many family members and advocates walked the halls to their representatives and delivered information about this bill and why they wanted it. Mark and I delivered my article and an information sheet before I testified at the Transportation meeting.

Testimony by the BRF board members, Paul Muller and myself, and AFSP field advocate Todd Handler was provided in both the California Assembly Transportation and Appropriation committees, sharing information that suicide is impulsive, people will reconsider their thoughts when they're provided time, few go on to die by suicide after an attempt, the cost factor of suicide and attempted suicide, and the impact on families and communities. Many families were present and spoke during the public comment time at each of these meetings.

I testified again for BridgeRail Foundation along with the representative from NAMI California in the State Senate Transportation Committee. It was here the essence of the bill was called upon. Shortly after losing Matt, I met with the committee chairman, Senator Mark DeSaulnier and we discussed suicides, bridges, and barriers. Senator DeSaulnier knows the grief that suicide brings as he lost his father by suicide and has been public about it. During our discussion in 2008, it was revealed that suicide barriers had not been discussed in the construction of the new eastern span of the Oakland Bay Bridge. During the transportation committee meeting, in 2013 I said:

> *Mr. Chairman, I was in your office shortly after losing my son and we discussed suicide bridges and barriers. We know the Oakland Bay Bridge has a history of over 150 suicides and most jumps from it are fatal. It would've been a good thing if AB 755 had been in place when the design phase began. It wasn't. Now we have a pedestrian and bicycle walkway with a railing that is just four and a half feet high. As disturbing as that is, I discovered just*

*last week that benches were installed. These benches are seven-
teen inches high, which effectively diminishes the railing height
to 37 inches, lower than the railing on the Golden Gate Bridge.
People now have easier access and less restriction to jump from
the Oakland Bay Bridge than ever before. This is the reason this
bill is essential.*

I was impressed when Senator Beall, who is an advocate for
mental health, leaned forward and questioned the facts about
the Oakland Bay Bridge walkway. Assembly member Ammiano
was quick to respond, comparing the Bay Bridge to its sister, the
Golden Gate Bridge. When the session was finished, Mr. Ammiano
walked to where I was seated, shook my hand, and thanked me. A
few months later, the bill was signed into law. I was proud to have
assisted in this lifesaving legislation.

In January 2014, BridgeRail Foundation members, volunteer
families, and recent survivors of suicide loss met on the steps of
San Francisco City Hall for a press conference to report the record
number of suicides from the previous year. Retired Marin County
coroner, Ken Holmes, said that in 2013, there were forty-six confirmed suicides at the Golden Gate Bridge, the highest number in a
year he can ever remember. Nicolas Aparicio's seventeen-year-old
daughter, Gabriela, became one of ten confirmed suicide victims
who jumped from the Golden Gate Bridge in August, the most suicides the bridge has seen in a month since its completion in 1937.

Four months later, the Golden Gate Bridge BOD voted unani-
mously to support and fund the suicide net, identifying the allocation
of money from the California Department of Transportation, the
MTC, the GGB district, and the state's mental health program.

By December of 2026, the net is expected to be completed.

From the beginning of this ordeal, my focus was recovering my
son and when I realized that would not be possible, it became creating a memorial for all the victims; all of those lost over the years.
It was something that I had discussed with Ken Holmes the first

time I met him. There are a few memorials for those lost at sea in San Francisco, the Fishermen's and Seamen's Chapel and the Lone Sailor memorial at the Vista Point on the north side of the bridge. Neither of these represents the victims of suicide, recovered or not.

Over the years, I've actively been searching for names of the victims through internet searches that can access public databases. My goal is to ensure that every name, every life is recognized by the time the net is in place and the suicides stop. Each of these names represents the life of a child, a sibling, a spouse, or a parent.

Dana Barks, who lost her son, Donovan, ran a healing ceremony for several years. These evolved into an event called "Names in the Sand." It is a time of reflection, of sharing our thoughts, our feelings, and our time together. Throughout the day people would take small scrolls with names of suicide victims and walk to the beach. At the tide's edge, we wrote the first names of every victim we knew. It is meant to be symbolic: the names in the sand exist only to be washed away by the waves, just as our loved ones existed only to be lost beneath the waves.

Over the years, on Matthew's angel-versary, I try to stop at the Bridge District Patrol office, the California Highway Patrol office in Marin, and the US Coast Guard office at Fort Baker in Sausalito. I deliver food or flowers with letters of thanks for everything they did trying to find and save my son and the countless others.

It must be difficult for these first responders to find a lifeless body or to lose a person you are trying to save after searching the waters, knowing families are hoping for the best outcome. I wanted them to know their efforts are very appreciated. The Coast Guard personnel remember each event, just like the families. They relive those memories with every new request for a search, and another, and another. It is post-traumatic stress and it takes its toll on everyone. Suicide goes beyond the victim and their family and friends. It has its own ripple effect on first responders, emergency room staff, coworkers of the victim, and families, friends of friends—everyone hearing about it, empathizing, and helpless to help.

A few years ago, I was contacted by the family who lost a sibling over forty years ago. They let me know that not a day goes by without thinking of him, and they love and miss him dearly. Their pain was rekindled by a recent loss in their community of a kind and caring man who died the same way as their brother. It reopened their wounds and led them to start searching the internet for answers. They found my website for Matthew and reached out.

I will continue to gather the names, work toward creating a memorial, and advocate for suicide prevention and reduction of stigma about mental illness. Some days are harder than others, but every success means another family will not endure what we have and will endure for our lifetime. That gives me some sense relief and peace.

When I would tell Matthew "...it only takes one person to make a difference." he didn't agree. Yet when there are hundreds or thousands of single voices coming together, they can make a change. It was not what I wanted, to lose Matthew by suicide to make a difference in our world.

But I stand by the words I told him. Mark and I made a small difference, but there are many more making a difference, using our voices to improve mental health awareness and suicide prevention in our lives and our communities.

Peace out, Mattie.

—**Dayna Whitmer** and **Mark**, in spirit
Mother and father of Matthew, missing since November 15, 2007
BridgeRail Foundation board member

CHAPTER 12

Being Patrick Lawson

Making great friends during my travels, and the making of our first documentary has been incredible. When I met this next character, I knew we'd be brothers for life. Our next contributing author, Patrick Lawson, shares his empowering and impactful story.

Patrick Lawson

I never thought mental illness and suicide would have such an impact on my life as it has to date. It all started for me in February of 2015. I was on my typical twenty-minute drive to work at roughly 6:30 in the morning. I was all but there when I felt a horrible pain in my stomach, and I had a sudden need to throw up. After swallowing a couple of big gulps of air to try and keep down whatever wanted to leave my body, I arrived at my workplace. No sooner had I pulled into the carpark that I had to run straight to the men's toilets and release this horrible demon that was building up.

I finished, wiped my face, walked out, and before I had the chance to say g'day to one of my fellow workers, I was back in there again releasing what felt like the spawn of the demon I had released earlier. This continued two more times. It was at that point I basically thought I had "gastro" and before I could turn and say to my workmate, "I can't be here," he sent me home. I got just past the front gates on my way home when I felt that horrible need again, but this time there was nothing. As I continued my twenty-minute drive home, my stomach started feeling better (weird). So, I made an appointment with my doctor that afternoon, to which he told me it was "a mild case of gastro" and proceeded to write me a doctor's note for that day and the following.

That's where it all went wrong. The following day, I said goodbye to my wife and kids for the morning as they went to work and day care. I didn't realize at the time that was potentially the last time I was going to see them, and that extra-long cuddle I had given them that morning was quite possibly the last one I was ever going to give them. I said my goodbyes.

Unbeknownst to them and unbeknownst to me, it was my final goodbye. You see, I had been fighting with my own head for way too long. I didn't know how to tell anyone that I was having personal problems. They would probably just tell me to "get over it" or say, "You'll be alright." or think I was seeking attention. (I love to have attention and all my family and friends know this.) But this was way more than that. I was at a point where I constantly hated myself; little things like getting out of bed or even getting to sleep at night seemed impossible some days.

Why does life hate me? or *What have I done to deserve this shit?* Were just a couple of the many thoughts I had in my head. The biggest one that had screamed at me a lot (especially recently) was, *They will be better off without you* and *They could use the money from your death more than they can use you.* Thoughts like this used to scare the absolute crap out of me. But they were thoughts that I had come so close to actioning so many times on my drive to and from work. *I could just veer left or right at the correct time and I won't have any more to worry about and my family will have the money they need.*

Cara [my wife] will find someone better and he will treat the kids like angels, like they should be treated. Not yelled at constantly for no reason, like I have been doing. But I never went through with it. Not until this day at home.

It was Tuesday, February 3, 2015, and I remember it vividly. As I said, I had said my goodbyes to everyone and now it was time to go. Time to go and remove all these thoughts and rid my amazing family of the nuisance I thought I had become.

I was ready to take my life…

It was at that point I proceeded to write my wife, Cara, a text message on the same phone where I had searched YouTube. A short message was all I needed to send, something simple to explain to her just how much I loved her and our kids and that none of this was her fault. It was simply the only solution for the pain in my head to "disappear" finally.

So here I was, ready to "rid" myself of the constant arguments, ready to "rid" my children and wife of a constantly angry husband and father and, mostly, ready to find the peace I had been looking for, for so, so long. All I had to do was press "send" on my phone and the job was finished. Then…COLD SHIVERS! I remember them running straight down my spine. (Like when you are telling a spooky story.) I remember looking down at my phone and reading the message I had just typed: "Cara, please don't hate me. Please don't blame yourself. This is something that needs to be done and you guys will be better off. I PROMISE. Please remember, I love you, Charlotte, and Thomas, more than the world and I will see you soon. I LOVE YOU. xxx"

"What are you bloody doing?"and "Get down, you bloody dickhead." Two statements I vividly remember hearing myself say. So, I did just that. I got down, and I thought about things for a minute. Something just stopped me from going through with this. What was it? *Who* was it? I don't know. But I can honestly say that I'm forever grateful that whatever or whoever was watching over me that day, saw what I was doing, and stopped it from happening. From that point, all I could do was cry. *A lot*. I never knew someone had so many tears in their body.

I made my way back into my backyard and onto my veranda and just *cried*. It's all I could seem to do. I was still feeling worthless, even more at the fact that I couldn't even kill myself—that's how useless I was. So, I cried, and I cried.

The rest of the day passed by quickly. Before I knew it, my wife and kids were home from school and day care, and I could barely pull myself out of the chair to say hello to them. I mustered up just enough to lean over and give them a kiss, and then I slumped back in my deck chair and continued to think about everything again. I vividly remember Cara asking me, "Is everything okay?" My eyes were red, and my cheeks were stained from the tears, and yet I still managed to say, "Yep. I'm fine. Don't worry. It's all good." It was at that moment I realized I needed to talk. I walked into the kitchen, grabbed my wife, and hugged her harder than a grizzly. I told her we needed to talk and that we should wait for the kids to go to bed, but it was too much, and I had to sit her down. We sat there for ages before I had the courage to open up. How do you tell the love of your life that you have tried to take your own life?

Finally, I said three words that, at that time, I never realized *would change my life*! I. Need. Help. I explained everything. My attempt, and all the intense fighting with my own head. *Everything*!

We then chatted about ways of getting through this. But first, I had to go to work the next day. I got to work the next day after about an hour of sleep that night. It also took a lot longer to get there, too, because I was so afraid of the way my head had been treating me.

But when I got there, I explained to my manager, Sheryl, what had happened, and we both went and saw our supervisor, Doug. I chatted with him for quite some time. We then discussed what I needed to do. I made my doc's appointment ASAP and was fortunate enough to get in at 9:30 that morning. Cara drove me the twenty-minute trip back into Corowa to see my GP, and after a long discussion and many questions I was diagnosed with clinical depression and anxiety.

From this came the hard parts. I was given a prescription for some antidepressants and a referral to see a psychologist. The only thing was that the meds take roughly two weeks to kick in and I couldn't see my psych for those same two weeks. I was beyond nervous.... Two more weeks of living with this hell! I contacted a local community organization about a possible mental health hub, which I might be able to attend, and I was told that the closest community program is about forty minutes away. *Awesome!* A suicidal man behind the wheel of a car—not a very good mix.

I was, however, very fortunate to have a good mate that I knew I could turn to. Someone who I never thought I would be so close to in the future, Joe Williams. I had been reading all about Joe and his struggles and battles with bipolar depression and his own suicide attempt. So, who better to contact than the man himself? We caught up for a coffee and had a great chat about life and everything associated with it, and he helped me to understand a great deal about myself and mental health in general. One thing I really took away from our chat is that I will never beat this. This is now a part of my life and I need to learn to manage it daily.

The following Monday came around. I had a massive anxiety attack at work and found myself in the hospital that afternoon. I was released later that evening and that was the moment I used Facebook to open up and tell my friends what I was going through. It was by far one of the best things I had done. The amount of love, compassion, and mostly support I was receiving was astounding. People were amazed that I had been diagnosed with it. I was always the fun, outgoing guy. Some others saw that I'd been struggling. The best part of reaching out was that now I knew I had a support network. It made my day.

I was given the next six to eight weeks off work to try to get myself "better." In that time, I read books, I saw my psychiatrist, then my meds kicked in and I learned to love life again. Oh. I also joined Tupperware and I had been asked by a close friend to do a talk about my mental illness at a day designated to raise money for Beyond Blue, an incredible suicide prevention and mental health organization here in Australia. I couldn't help but jump at the chance. I got up and spoke about what I had been through, and I had everyone's attention. It was great to see so many people wanting to hear about something that had so often been swept under the rug. After six weeks off work, it was time to return. I was back in the workforce, but it didn't seem the same. Maybe, I had been away for too long and realized what sort of a place I was working for. I started to notice a lot of things. I also started feeling like they were trying to get rid of me. Maybe my anxiety was playing up. I don't know, but something was different. A few weeks after being back, I couldn't handle the place anymore and I left and started concentrating on my Tupperware.

I was pretty good at selling this stuff. I loved that I was the only male in our region, and I loved the amazing people I got to see and meet on a weekly basis. But mostly, I was loving life again. I was fortunate to have amazing directors in Graham and Rebecca Bullock, and they were helping me so much with everything I needed help with. I remember sitting at a sales meeting one Monday night and hearing them say, "Tupperware's conference is on this weekend in Melbourne; let your manager know if you want to come."

I had a good chat with my manager (my oldest sister Catherine) and told her, "I would love to go, but I just can't afford it." She insisted and told me to stay in her room for the night. So, I did. It was awesome, such an eye opener. One thousand plus people, crammed into a room, yelling and screaming with excitement. Oh. I also got to go on stage a few times too. Ha ha. The day ended and with that, I had to drive three hours back to Corowa. I had all these amazing ideas in my head. I was pumped. I had a party the next day and I had so many things I wanted to do and share.

The next day I went to my party still pumped up and ready to rock. Sales were low, which was fine. But I got to show off all the new stuff. It was awesome. My adrenaline levels were through the roof until the next day. I had come down like a sack of bricks. I had no party the next day and no one to share my news with. I was in one of the lowest places I had been in a while. It was the start of August, Monday the third, and I was stuck in bed. I couldn't bring myself to get up and face the day. I was feeling so low. Nothing could help me. Then, I remembered something Joe had taught me. "Look at pics of quotes and family when you're feeling down, mate. It really does help." So, I reached for my phone and went to my gallery. Just as I went to hit the album, my finger had pressed the camera button and I found myself staring at myself.

Suddenly, I started talking. I started to be honest about my feelings and life in general. I was staring at myself, having a good old chat. I look back now and realize I was doing this because there I was, with all my problems, talking and opening up to myself. I was on the other side, listening and not judging. It was enough to make me take the next step and get out of bed. It was at that moment that I put an idea out there on Facebook about starting a page to help my friends who were going through a similar thing. I was given the green light to do it, and it was at that point that 3 Words; I Need Help Facebook page was born.

It was somewhere for mates to go with candor and chat about their life and problems and not worry about getting any negativity thrown at them. I started by inviting my friends to the page and then they started inviting their friends and so on and so forth. Next thing I knew, fifteen hundred people were on this page I created to help my mates. Then sixteen hundred, then seventeen hundred, and now it's global. What then? With this global success of the page came a trip to Tumut High School to help educate students on mental illness. I had made it into the newspapers a few times, and it was amazing. *Life was amazing!*

I still remember this next part as clearly as any other day in my life. I was sitting at my parents (John and Vicki Lawson) in Wagga Wagga. I was flicking through Facebook and a Buzzfeed video came into view. Some guy had attempted to take his own life by jumping off the Golden Gate Bridge and survived? I had to watch it. This man's name is Kevin Hines—well, you know, this is his anthology book you are reading right now, and his story is a part of my chapter. I was absolutely amazed by his story. This guy is one of the most inspirational people I have ever come across. Wow. I remember him saying at the end of his video. "Leave a short 2 min video about how suicide has caused a ripple effect in your life" and "and what you're doing to help others." So, I headed over to the Suicide: The Ripple Effect Facebook page and proceeded to make a quick video. A couple of weeks went by, and I was very busy with my life and my page until one day I saw a friend request from a guy named Greg Dee. *Who's this? Greg Dee. I don't know a Greg Dee*, so I did the usual Facebook stalk and saw that he was tied up with some documentary titled *Suicide: The Ripple Effect.*

I thought that was just a page. It was a documentary, cool... Next thing, *bing bing*, friend request...*Kevin Hines*...Kevin *freaking* Hines wanted to be my friend. Holy crap. This was huge. Usually, it was me chasing after famous people. Accept, accept. We were now friends. Time to stalk. Wow. Kevin was in Sydney doing filming for the doco. I wondered if he was coming down to Melbourne. It was a bit closer, and I wanted to meet him in person. I asked. The next minute, my bloody phone rang for a Facebook phone call. It was Kevin Hines. *The* Kevin Hines was calling me... What the actual F@&#!

After a good chat for about half an hour and constantly pinching myself, I got off the phone and ran to Cara to tell her the awesome news. "Cara, Kevin Hines just called me and has asked me to be a part of his *global* doco." I was so gobsmacked I couldn't even get my words out properly. After going backward and forward through messages and getting to add some amazing people and new Aussie pals to my friends list, I noticed someone else's name. Joe Williams was a part of this, too. This couldn't be more awesome. I was fortunate enough to meet a few of the amazing people from #TeamRippleAus in Sydney in December 2015 when we got together for our first film shoot. They are amazing people, and I am forever grateful to be able to call them family. We then caught up once again in January for more filming, after which I was asked to go onto ABC News to tell my story.

We were all asked to go to Las Vegas for NATCON16 (National Council for Mental Wellbeing Conference), now called the National Council for Mental Well-Being). After six days in Vegas and three at NATCON and getting to meet some absolutely amazing individuals doing amazing things in the mental health and suicide prevention industries, I realized something.

I have found my calling in life. I now know what I need to be doing with my life. I need to be helping other people from this point on. I am currently studying for my diploma in mental health. I'm also networking with some amazing people and working on getting on the Suicide Prevention Australia ambassadors program. I am working on getting into school and helping spread this message and wanting to really focus on mental health in men, youth, and regional Australia. The world is my oyster and I wish I had more time to thank all the people that have been such amazing influences on my life and helped me to get to where I am today. In closing, I would like to finish with a quote that was shown to me at the start and one that still sticks very heavily in my heart: "If you can't fly, then run. If you can't run, then walk. If you can't walk, then crawl. But whatever you do, don't stop moving forward."—Martin Luther King Jr.

—**Patrick Lawson**, 3 Words founder, mental health champion

CHAPTER 13

Being Jas Rawlinson

Our next contributing author seems to give back all day every day; hers is a story of giving not to receive, but only to be of service to others. Purpose is what drives Jas Rawlinson. She lived through and survived domestic violence. The terrible experiences she lived with shape her current advocacy, and her intense struggle led to her life's purpose, helping to save lives through suicide prevention and the work she does daily.

Jas Rawlinson

The roof was warm, its gunmetal gray panels barely moving as I hoisted myself upwards onto the top of the horse shed. From there, I could swivel my view to the right, taking in the sight of the paddocks that ran all the way to the train tracks at the end of the road. And then, beyond them, a vast expanse of dense, woody forest.

If I listened carefully enough, I could still hear the laughter and shouts of my school mates; the hundreds of teenagers who were, right now, enjoying lunch just a mere fifty meters up the road.

But I didn't want to be with them. I didn't want to be around anyone. All I wanted was to be away from the hell that lived inside my brain 24/7—the anxiety that swirled within the tight walls of my tiny sixteen year old body and the questions that swarmed my mind.

What time will Dad get home from work today?
What kind of mood is he going to be in?
Is he going to make me pay for speaking up for myself last night?

Sitting on the hot tin roof, knees pulled inwards, I thought about that look; the one that burned deep within Dad's eyes whenever Dr. Jekyll went away…the look that told us Mr. Hyde had come to play again and again and again.

For the past eight years, I'd been living in a home where my mother, brother, and I were at the mercy of Dad's emotional and verbal abuse, and my ability to cope was wearing thin. Walking around the playground, I often felt as though some invisible "thing" was pulling down the corners of my mouth and squishing my stomach in its hands. The sadness was overwhelming; the self-hatred soul-destroying.

Some mornings on the way to school, he'd berate me about how it was "all my fault" that he'd been fighting with Mum, and that if they divorced it would be all because of me. Other days, he told me I was stupid, would "never amount to anything," and that I deserved to be "sent away to a home for bad girls." On another more terrifying night, I watched as his face contorted into pure violence and he lunged toward me, trying desperately to grab the cordless phone from my hand before I could call the police. Heart thundering, I sprinted to the driveway and dialed emergency, begging—through broken sobs—for someone to come and help us.

Sadly, by the time they arrived my dad had transformed back into his charming alter ego. To my absolute humiliation, he turned to the police officer and told them to focus on me instead. "You should be investigating her. She abuses her little brother."

Me? An abuser?

The lie gutted me, the force of it leaving me with a sense of injustice that felt physically painful. Because nothing could have been further than the truth. The truth was that I was a shy, sensitive kid—the kind who never wanted to upset or hurt anyone. I studied hard, and the only times I went out were for sleepovers at my girlfriends' houses or the occasional movie. I didn't drink or do drugs, yet nothing I did was good enough. Any time I achieved something good in my life or experienced a sense of freedom and fun (like a weekend with friends), he'd make sure he ruined it for me.

Worst of all, though, was having to watch on helplessly as he screamed and berated my mother, accusing her of all kinds of awful untruths. All I wanted was to protect her, but I couldn't. And as I grew older and tried to begin standing up to him more, the danger only grew worse for Mum and me.

So here I was, sitting on the top of a giant horse shed in our school's agricultural plot, trying to forget about it all. If I'm honest, I did dream of death. Of taking actions that would remove me from this painful world. But all I really wanted was for the violence at home to stop.

I stood up, and began walking carefully along the tin sheets, peering down at the ground below. Then, suddenly, I saw something that made my heart quicken. The sight of a teacher and a group of students walking down the road toward me.

Shit.

I scrambled down from the roof, trying to hide. But it was too late. I'd already been spotted. Understandably my teacher was concerned, but for me, all I felt was embarrassment. Embarrassment that I was now being escorted back to the school grounds by a girl several years younger than me, as if I were some helpless, feeble person. Embarrassment that they thought I was going to kill myself. I remembered the way my teacher's face fell when I scoffed, "If I was going to kill myself, I'd pick a higher roof."

The truth was, I did want to die. But I couldn't tell my teacher. I couldn't tell anyone.

I knew I was unraveling. I just didn't know how long it would take for all the pieces of yarn that stitched together the fabric of my soul to finally fly away in the next violent storm; a storm that forever circled the four walls I called "home."

At age eighteen, I was sliding into a deep and unyielding darkness. One I wasn't sure I would ever escape from. Over the past few months my depression and suicidality had only grown worse, and so too had Dad's abuse. He was a ticking time bomb, and none of us knew how long it would be until he did something truly horrific. Would we become the next news statistic?

In desperation, I called the number of a family friend who had once provided us with a "safe house" to escape to for six months, rent free, when I was seventeen. With the phone pressed close to my ear, my voice hushed, I asked if she and her husband—who had been developing a number of properties—had any more houses that we could disappear to.

"I'm so sorry Jas," she said, her voice laden with regret. "We sold the development earlier this year."

Instantly, a wave of despair washed over me. I was alone. This nightmare was never going to end. *There's no way out*, it screamed.

Turning to my journal, I scrawled a mess of words, a narrative of hatred and fear and sadness. "I just wish he would disappear forever," I wrote. As I did, I pictured my dad's face. The way he'd sneered at me the day before, his middle finger raised as I yelled out, "I hate you!" ("I hate you too" was his reply.)

The date of my journal entry was January 3rd, 2004. You might be wondering how it is that I can remember. Well, as I soon discovered, this was a date that I would look back on for months to come. The eve of something unexpected. Something I never could have imagined.

If I had only known what was about to happen, maybe I never would have written that diary note.

On January 4, in the late afternoon, I walked toward the car park, scanning for my mother's car. But instead, I saw my neighbor waiting for me. Minutes later came the news.

Dad was dead.

No. No, this is just some kind of joke. I panicked. *Suicide? What... why...? No. Just no.*

A sound somewhere between laughter and disbelief and shock escaped my mouth. I didn't know how to react. What to say. How to feel.

No. This was not meant to happen. Not like this. Not like this...

Trying to describe how I felt in the wake of everything that happened on January 4, 2004, is still traumatic.

Though I was not responsible for his actions, I couldn't help but feel that I'd caused Dad's death. My head was a mixture of shock, guilt, relief, and devastation. A cacophony of broken sentences starting with, "This is all my fault," and ending with, "But I don't miss him. Why do I not miss him?"

For a decade, all I'd wanted was for Dad to disappear. For the abuse to stop. And now, finally, it had. The problem was the emotions I now experienced weren't the ones I'd longed for. I didn't feel free. I didn't feel at ease. I didn't feel happy. I didn't feel anything I thought I would.

I was still trapped in a void of hopelessness with no sense of direction.

It should come as no surprise that, at the tender age of eighteen, I entered adulthood as a very emotionally damaged young woman with a toxic mixture of trauma and insufficient coping strategies. A mixture that would, inevitably, lead me into a world of poor life choices and further trauma.

For the next two years, I played with fire, putting myself in risky situations, giving my heart to emotionally unavailable and uncaring men who pushed me into doing things I didn't want to do and spending countless nights drinking and partying.

Did I consciously know that I was putting myself in unsafe environments? Did I recognize that the men I was infatuated with only wanted to use and discard me? Sometimes. But often not. Because to me, an abusive relationship was one in which a woman was hit or kicked or punched. And despite my own upbringing, I didn't recognize the complex warning signs and red flags of emotional abuse—let alone sexual coercion. More to the point, I didn't really care. I just wanted to feel something. Anything...yes, anything other than the numb, achy void that my antidepressants made me feel.

Eventually, the lifestyle I was living caught up with me, ending in the most traumatic moment of my life. A sexual assault at the hands of a man who I had known, trusted, and considered a friend for the previous eighteen months.

This was my wakeup call. A blaring alarm that I could no longer ignore. *You have to change, Jas. You can't stay this way. If you don't, something even worse will happen next time.*

A shiver of fear ran through my skin. It was inevitable that there would be a next time because I knew nothing good could come from continuing to live as a victim, from giving my power away to everyone else. I needed to transform. I needed to change. But how do you know where to start when you've never been shown the way? It's like trying to build a house with no tools, no qualifications, and no plan.

My journey out of victimhood started slowly. At first, I made a list of all the qualities I wanted in a potential partner, and what I needed most in life—things like safety, love, respect, and honesty. Then I made a list of the things I would no longer tolerate, such as lies, broken promises, men who disrespected my boundaries or beliefs, and people who pressured me to keep drinking and partying.

When I entered a new relationship just a few months later, I was—understandably—fearful. Would he take advantage of me like every other guy? Would he betray my trust? I didn't know. What I did know, however, was that I could create boundaries that gave me the best chance possible of thriving and staying safe. This meant that, instead of simply trusting whatever I was told, I made my new boyfriend show me that he could be trusted. When he made plans, did he show up on time? Did he stick to his promises and speak to me in ways that made me feel peaceful, supported, and respected? Were my boundaries important to him, and did the rest of his life and the relationships he had with friends and family match up with the way he treated me?

These were all important questions that I asked myself in the wake of my assault. They were small steps, but ones that were powerfully important. And as I began to see that he was a person who could be trusted, I began to feel more confident in speaking up and sharing about what I did and didn't want in a relationship.

As the years rolled by and I began to live a healthier, happier life, I found that many of the hurts of my past began to soften. However, just because life had dulled their sharp edges, it didn't mean they weren't still there. Addressing my trauma wasn't an option at this stage, and I had no interest in doing so. Instead, I pushed it away, locking it inside a treasure chest and dumping it into the darkest depths of my consciousness.

Out of sight, out of mind.

As I've since learned, trauma doesn't work that way.

You can't lock it away and just pretend that it's gone. You can't stomp on its inky black tentacles and push it into a box never again to be seen. It's a clever beast, one that knows how to pick the lock and break into your house when you least expect. It's like a text message from an ex, or a DM from a toxic old friend who you'd blocked, only to find that they'd made a new account just to contact you. *Hey, long time no chat! We should hang out sometime.*

For me, my trauma resurfaced almost a decade to the day after my sexual assault. By this stage I was doing well in life, and in my mind, there was no reason for any past memories to resurface. I'd married a wonderful man, had moved cities, and was establishing myself as a writer and respected advocate against social injustices such as domestic violence, child abuse, and human trafficking. Even more exciting was that I was preparing to open the first permanent domestic violence memorial in our city, and one of the first of its kind in Australia. It was something that my friend Bonnie and I had been working on for six months and a project that understandably held a lot of significance to me. In the leadup to the official opening—which would be filmed and shared by local TV and media networks—I'd been speaking with many women who had experienced, or lost a child to, domestic violence. Their stories broke my heart and tore at my soul. Yet, never once did I consider myself to be one of the survivors I was advocating so hard for.

Thank God I never had to experience anything like that. *I'm so lucky*, I'd think, as I spoke with women or men who'd lived through extreme physical or sexual violence. It was bizarre that I never once stopped to consider that the gaslighting, general "bad" behavior, and love bombing that I'd experienced were all components of domestic violence. (For context, love bombing is a tool often used by abusers, where they will overwhelm you with affection, gifts, or what appears to be "love" in order to control and dampen your perception of their abuse).

Had my abuser been a stranger in a dark alley, there would have been no question about calling his actions what they were—rape. Had he hit me, I would have automatically known that this was an abusive relationship. But because I considered him a friend and he'd refused to officially call me his girlfriend (even when we were dating), I didn't see his actions for what they were. As a friend said to me at the time, "Jas, you knew him. You dated him. So…it's not rape."

The leaps our mind will make to excuse these kinds of experiences is really quite astonishing. Yet, this is the truth. Take it from someone with lived experience.

It wasn't until I began to learn more about domestic violence and the fact that it can also include financial, religious, emotional, and sexual abuse, that my entire carefully constructed story collapsed.

As the memories began to resurface, tearing free from the treasure chest I'd stuffed them into years beforehand, my comfortable life began to fall apart. The thoughts tormented me at work, interrupting the mundane tasks I was working on. They followed me down the bicycle path outside the office, as I hid away under a leafy tree to eat alone—just me and my depression. And at night, they tore apart my mind with thorny questions and pointed accusations: *Why didn't you stop him? Why didn't you fight back? Why did you even go to his house that night? It wasn't rape. Was it rape? This is all your fault!*

Then the trauma went after the most important thing in my life—my marriage. Never once had I ever felt unsafe around my husband, until one night where—out of nowhere—a sudden trigger went off inside my body, sending me into flight mode.

In that moment, it was like a tap was turned on, and all the fear and pain came rushing out. It began with a gnawing uneasiness in my stomach, and a quickening of my breath, until suddenly I was gasping for air. My husband, immediately sensing that something was wrong, quietly, and calmly asked what was happening. But I couldn't answer. I could barely breathe, and the only words I could muster were, "Don't touch me!" (It's possible the words never even left my lips, but everything inside was screaming these three words.) I didn't want to be touched. My body wanted to transport itself one hundred kilometers away. All I wanted was the sensation of soft, safe, baggy fabric around my body; oversized sweatpants and shirts that swam around my limbs—clothing I would never usually wear.

I want to disappear.

I went from zero to "get me the hell out of this house" in sixty seconds.

This was the night that I finally realized I was experiencing Post Traumatic Stress (PTS).

As supportive and understanding as my husband was through that panic attack, I knew that I had to get help. I had to find a way to acknowledge and clear these traumatic memories because if I didn't, I knew they could do real damage to my marriage and my health.

Soon afterwards, I made an appointment with a local general practitioner and asked for a mental health care plan. This was a huge step, as I'd never once had a positive experience with a professional and didn't really want to share such intimate details with a stranger. But I had to try. Because the alternatives weren't any better.

In many ways, I got lucky; the psychologist I worked with ended up being just the right fit for me. She was professional, empathetic, and seemed to truly care. Together, we worked on some ideas for how I could begin to process, and move on from, the traumatic memories holding me back. Through our discussions, I discovered that the number one thing that was most traumatic wasn't the assault itself—it was the fact that no one in my abuser's circle of friends or family knew what he had done. Like most perpetrators, he was just living his life as "normal" with no one to hold him accountable.

For many of us who have experienced sexual abuse, the thought of going to the police—let alone facing our abuser in court—is an added level of trauma that we don't feel prepared to take on. As a result, we lack closure. There is no sense of justice; and for me, this was certainly the case.

"I'm never going to get closure from him...so I don't know what to do," I said to my psychologist.

"Have you thought of writing a letter of everything you wished you'd had the chance to say to him?" she asked gently.

"I could. But I don't know that that will give me the closure I need. I need to break the secrecy."

She thought for a moment. "What if you wrote to his family, or to his current partner?"

Quietly, I pondered, the silence between us stretching out. Something began to settle over me. At the same time, I was conflicted. The idea of telling his mother was crushing. I thought about the last conversation I'd had with her ten years prior; the shitty excuse I'd given as to why I'd stopped hanging out with her son. The lie that protected her heart as well as his abuse. But after ten years of keeping his secret, I just couldn't do it anymore.

Revealing the truth to my abuser's family was one of the bravest things I've ever done. It was painful and terrifying, but it was also the catalyst to breaking free from my PTS. Through the process of reaching out, I had to let go of any attachment to a specific outcome, and instead, just "accept." I had to stay grounded in the knowledge that this was about speaking my truth, whether it was heard or ignored. That was the goal.

Throughout this process I also went to a police station in my hometown and—with the help of a friend—reported the abuse. As I handed over photocopies of diary entries and evidence from a decade prior, I knew that I was taking a powerful step toward my healing. I was stepping up for the twenty-year-old girl who was too burdened with shame to do so before then. I was breaking the silence and refusing to uphold his reputation any longer. I was taking back my power and making sure there was something on record, should he ever do this to another woman. And above all, I was giving myself the power to move on—regardless of whether a single police officer believed me or not.

I never ended up mailing the letter I wrote to my abuser. In the end, I just didn't feel it was the right option. What was helpful, however, was writing down everything I wanted to say to him. All the angry, bitter words I'd never spoken. All the things I'd never had the guts to say as a twenty-year-old.

And when it was done and all out on paper, I could see the truth. I was safe. I had a beautiful life. His family and partner knew everything, and there was no reason for me to feel ashamed any longer. He hadn't destroyed me. I'd won.

To me, that was justice.

It has now been seven years since I stepped foot in that police station. Today, I live a life of safety, freedom, and (mostly) peace, and run a successful business as an award-nominated ghostwriter, book coach, and resilience speaker. My specialty? Storytelling that saves and changes lives.

When I look back at my past, I no longer feel shame, regret, or guilt; instead, I see the challenges and traumas I've experienced as stepping stones to creating a fulfilling life where I'm able to help others who are living in a place of hopelessness, overwhelm, or shame. Just as I once was. In the past four years, I've worked with close to thirty suicide and trauma survivors, supporting them to write, publish, and share their stories of triumph over adversity through my best-selling series *Reasons to Live: One More Day, Every Day*, and have been blessed to collaborate with incredibly humans— including the beautiful soul that is Kevin Hines.

I'm no longer that girl who sat on the rooftop of a horse shed, praying for death to save her from the pain of living another moment. I no longer live with relentless self-hatred that makes me want to stay within my comfort zone, never yearning or striving for more. I now live with purpose, inner fulfillment, and acceptance and love for who I am.

There are a number of things I do for my mental wellbeing and inner resilience, some of which are daily and others that are weekly. Below are a few of my staple favorites.

Gratitude Journaling

Some people think of writing and journaling as something that only high schoolers do for fun, but in reality, it's one of the best things we can do for our mental wellbeing. In fact, a 2016 study from Greater Berkley found that participants who wrote letters of gratitude experienced higher levels of happiness as well as greater activation and neural sensitivity in the medial prefrontal cortex, an area of the brain associated with learning and decision making. This also showed that people who are more grateful are often more attentive to how they express gratitude.

Speaking from personal experience, I've found that putting aside just a few minutes at the end of the day to list five things I'm grateful for is helpful in shifting my mindset from being stressed-out and crappy to being calmer and happier. Think of it as your daily wellness vitamin.

Digital Detoxing

I'm going to admit, right now, that I spend way too much time looking at my phone. And I know that it's not good for me. Not only does it increase my anxiety and tendency to compare myself to others, but it often activates my fight or flight response and creates havoc with my digestion.

Unfortunately, I'm not alone in this struggle. Overuse of technology is one of the biggest battles faced by young people today, and it's killing our creativity, inner peace, and ability to be present.

If you're looking to improve your wellbeing, one of the best things you can do is choose a day of the week to do a digital detox. It could be a Saturday or Sunday, or you might choose to start with half a day. Whatever you do, I recommend swapping screen time for a physical book, some time in the garden, a walk with a friend, or another hobby that gets you away from technology.

Make Time for *You*

I used to think of self-care as bubble baths or a nice meal with a glass of wine. But the reality is that these are just short-term fixes and, let's be honest, alcohol is not the best treatment for our mental or physical health.

True self-care is the type that nourishes you from the inside out and lasts long after the experience. It's a regular practice that builds upon itself, like Lego blocks, to create a strong foundation. For example, in late 2020, I realized that I was experiencing burnout several times per year—mostly because I never took time for myself. I was always busy, busy, busy, serving everyone else. Change only came when I prioritized myself enough to stop and ask what I needed.

For me, I'm happiest when I'm by the ocean. So, for the last year, I've rearranged my working week to include beach walks on a Friday. I've also become selfish about this, and no longer schedule work on those days. Thankfully I have wonderful clients who respect boundaries, but if I should ever have someone who doesn't, I feel confident to politely say: "Sorry, I'm not available that day."

Self-care isn't selfish—it's essential. After all, how can I serve others if I'm not filling my own cup first?

In the darkest of times and the moments where you feel this world is better off without you, remember there is always a reason to live, and there is always a spark of hope waiting to be found. Our traumas don't disappear overnight, but by choosing to live one more day, every day, we can find our way out of hopelessness and into hope.

And finally, if no one else tells you this today, hear it from me: You are stronger than you realize. You deserve good things. I love you and I'm cheering for you.

CHAPTER 14

Being Brandi Benson

Contributing author Brandi Benson is a combat veteran, a stellar author, a powerful public speaker, and a personal hero of mine. She stays true to her roots as well, keeping those who have helped her close and within reach of gratitude.

Surviving the Wars—At Home, Internally, and for Our Country: Brandi Benson

From a very young age, I was taught that being vulnerable was disruptive and unwanted behavior. This lesson was not taught by my parents but by the many elementary schools I was kicked out of at the age of seven.

Looking back at it, this is where I had my first mental health decline, at seven years old. I was having manic depressive episodes coupled with uncontrollable crying fits because my family had been ripped apart, and my guttering sobs and emotions were just too much for my little self to contain. I would cry during my entire class only for my teachers to kick me out and tell me to hold it in until

I got home. Then I'd be made fun of by my peers and called "the Crybaby."

This experience set the tone for my mental health and how I dealt with feelings of abandonment. I eventually grew stone-faced and unmoved by others' needs—especially their grief. The shame I carried from being made fun of at school stained my brain and leaked over into all my relationships, especially with men. With every painful experience of abandonment, my heart became colder and colder, and the little girl in me overshadowed my ability to be vulnerable as I grew older. I'd created an alter ego to protect myself. Problem was, I was becoming too tough and out of touch with reality. I became a cold bitch.

Here's the story...

My parents split when I was six years old. My mother had grown tired of my father abusing drugs and alcohol. On top of being an addict, he was also schizophrenic, so he could see people that we couldn't. He explained that they wore vests that would make them invisible to us. Well, he decided that he would get rid of them once and for all. He dropped my mom off at work, convinced the invisible people to get in the car, drove them ten miles away, then walked home. When it came time to pick my mom up, he walked to get her. She asked about the car, and he told her that he had to leave it behind so the people couldn't follow him back home. Then there was the time he stabbed the wall with a broom, leaving a huge hole, to save someone from falling into the wall. In another instance, he started sleeping with a dinner plate on his chest to protect himself from being stabbed in the heart. It was a lot for my mother to handle. Hell, it was a lot for anyone.

No one talked about mental health back then, though. I now recognize these symptoms as delusions, hallucinations, paranoia, and inappropriate emotional responses. He had trouble distinguishing between what was real and what was imagined. Back then, though, everyone just assumed he must have been possessed by the Devil.

In fact, my mom took him to her sister in California to have an exorcism performed on him. It seemingly worked, for a little while. When his episodes returned, my mother decided that enough was enough. How could my father be the provider that we all needed if he couldn't even help himself? The day she left him was the same day that he decided that he was keeping me with him.

She stuck to her plan of moving and went on to California with my sister and stepfather. It's not that she didn't care about me. She just figured that it was better to call my dad's bluff than to fight him. I ended up staying with him for about a year before I reunited with my mother. In that year, my father and I moved from Oregon to his hometown in southern California (Victorville). He was my father, so I didn't feel kidnapped, but I knew something wasn't right. Where were my mother and sister, and why couldn't I see them? Why couldn't I live with them? That confusion quickly turned to anger. I felt abandoned and unwanted. Seven years old is a pivotal age. Children are starting to crave acceptance and think about the future. Let alone being accepted by peers, I felt that I wasn't even accepted by my own mother. Would she ever come back for me? I had endless questions with no answers, and that was incredibly terrifying and frustrating. There was no therapy, though. My father's mental illness wasn't being treated or even addressed, so my traumatic experiences most certainly were not.

I wasn't allowed to talk to my mom for many months. He feared that if I did, then I'd tell her where I was, and she'd come get me (or even get law enforcement involved). I switched schools several times because I kept getting kicked out for disrupting class with outbursts. In addition to abandonment issues and their consequent grief, I also took out my anger on classmates. I would terrorize the boys in my class to release the anger and powerlessness that I felt at home but couldn't express. By age seven, children can usually get along well without their parents; they're beginning to establish a sense of independence. That's the case with children who come from grounded, secure backgrounds. For childhoods mirroring mine, that's not the case. A seven-year-old raised in unstable environments can act very much like a toddler because that's how they feel. You feel as needy and uncertain of the world as a two-year-old who hasn't gotten the hang of the fact that you're dropped off then picked up and the pattern repeats. I always feared I'd be left or forgotten.

Moving to California helped, and my school situation was better. I had a cousin there and Aunt Julie, my father's sister, was one of my teachers who'd become somewhat of a mother figure to me. I was even allowed to start talking to my mom again. The rule was that I couldn't let her know where I was, though. He coached me on what I could and couldn't say. I was so desperate to talk to her again and was still the obedient child at home that I'd always been, so I happily obliged. He'd monitor the calls to make sure that I didn't break the rule. One day, she asked me what school I went to. I didn't know that I wasn't allowed to tell her the truth. I just knew I wasn't supposed to say where I was, who I was living with, or what city I was in. Just as casually as she'd asked, I answered. "Get off the phone!" he screamed. I got off the phone, completely shaken. What did I do wrong? I didn't break the rule. He hung up on her then stormed into my room. "Why would you do that? Do you want her to take you away from me? Now she's gonna come and get you. She doesn't love you. She left you."

To be abandoned by your mother, by the person whose voice you heard first and whose heartbeat you felt for the first forty or so weeks of your life does significant psychological damage. Although my mother did want me, I didn't know that, so the effects were the same. Self-esteem is affected, as is your ability to trust others and even yourself. As a result, your moods swing faster than you can keep up with. Your peers don't seem to be experiencing the depression and anxiety that you are, so now you feel even further alienated.

My plot twisted yet again when I was called to the principal's office one day. I thought it was for fighting, but I had a visitor. My mother was there with the sheriff and Uncle Brian. She had loads of paperwork and toys. While driving away, I asked if I could say bye to my dad. She turned around and said, "You'll never see him again." I shrugged it off and resumed playing with my new toys. It's not that I didn't want to see my dad again. I loved him, looked just like him. I was a daddy's girl. I loved them both, but I didn't exactly understand what she was saying. After all, my dad led me to believe that I'd never see my mom again, and that obviously wasn't true. So, I dismissed it and basked in the glory of finally reuniting with my mom and sister.

My mother was serious about me never talking to my father or anyone on his side of the family again, however. I wasn't even allowed to talk about them. I was told that if I wanted to speak to them again, I'd have to wait until I was eighteen. She feared that he might come and take me away and put me in hiding again. It is truly a parent's nightmare to have one of your kids taken away by the other parent. Looking back in hindsight, I truly understand her logic. She was trying to protect me, but the collateral damage was already done. The seeds of abandonment and war were being watered.

My father found a way around that, though. When I was about thirteen, he called our house. He disguised his voice to sound like a child, then relaxed his tone after learning that it was me on the phone. Excitement is an understatement. He warned me that I couldn't tell anyone that he'd called, and I graciously agreed. We mapped out a plan to be together again. When I turned eighteen, I'd move back in with him (and I couldn't wait).

I didn't know that would be the last time I'd ever talk to my father again. He died when I was sixteen, and I was devastated! Now my father was dead and I didn't even get a chance to say goodbye. I later learned that he never stopped looking for my sister and me. Then came the next blow to my spirit when my stepfather abandoned us. We didn't have the best relationship, considering he was very impatient and often rude with me, but he provided a level of comfort and consistency that I wasn't used to. He and my sister were very close. She even called him Dad. Now he was gone, and he'd left us in Hawaii with not an inkling of financial support. Overnight, it seemed, we went from being a middle-class family to an extremely poor one.

We had no money and no food and were forced to live off military MREs (meals ready to eat) for months. Our dogs were starving, the lights were getting cut off, cars were getting repossessed. We went through a really rough time trying to survive. My mother worked endless hours and no matter how creative my mom got with saving or earning money, it was never enough. Of course, this was not her fault; no one saw this coming. This abandonment forced me to grow up fast. It also solidified me into one cold-ass bitch. I didn't have the luxury of concerning myself with school gossip, the latest fashion, or trying to be prom queen. I didn't even feel I had space to worry about myself. My mother and my sister were drowning emotionally. Meanwhile, I felt far more anger than sadness. Every bit of rage that I felt as a child resurfaced. I couldn't take it out on classmates this time, though. I also wasn't as powerless as I was then either, so I decided to channel those feelings by stepping up to the plate to save us. Whenever children are forced to grow up fast, they are often stuck with this lingering notion that they have to always be strong, can't ask for help, and that somehow, acknowledging their pain makes them weak. I felt all of this on top of the abandonment I'd struggled with since age seven and the grief I was forced to suppress after my father died.

What I wanted to be when I grew up was no longer just about me. I wanted to take care of my family because I knew that I'd never abandon us. They could depend on me to be there. I just had to figure out a way to make it happen, so I revisited my childhood dream of joining the military. I was always competitive, strong, fast, and flexible. I grew up wanting to do something that would challenge my body as much as my mind. Well, we lived right outside of a military base in Hawaii, and all my friends were military. Their parents were the ones dropping off the MREs and helping us. With Uncle Sam, I figured, we would never have to suffer again.

I did exactly what I set out to do, except there was more suffering around the corner. A lot more. My sister joined the military first, then I did at twenty-four years old. I was in basic training for three months, AIT for two months, then I went to my main duty station for one month and nine days when I was told that I was getting shipped out to Iraq…to war. What the hell?! I had just learned how to shoot an M16, throw a grenade, clear the room, determine if a lung was punctured, insert the catheter between certain ribs, and so on. Now I was being sent off to turn the green grass red. I barely paid attention because I didn't think I was going so soon. Yet, there I was in 2008, flying to Iraq, leaving the life I knew worlds away. I immediately regretted my decision to enlist; I remember experiencing the feelings of great despair and doom. I felt sick to my stomach when I landed in theater. I was this college girl who was now among real killers—snipers. I'd also gotten married that year to a guy named Q, whom I'd fallen in love with back in Hawaii.

He played for a popular traveling basketball competition and was quiet and mysterious, which made me want to get to know him. He was attractive too. My favorite thing about him was how athletic he was. His potential also drew me in. If he would just stay straight and do what he had to do, I thought, he could have a great future playing professional basketball. That was difficult for him though. He grew up in public housing and was used to living the fast life, spending money as quickly as he made it. He'd self-sabotage by missing practice, tryouts, and flights. I so badly wanted to help him because I'm a fixer. At that time, we believed that to stay together in the military, you had to get married. So we did.

If I thought life was hectic before my deployment, the pressure quadrupled afterwards. We were in this place called FOB Echo in Diwaniyah, which is one hundred and something miles south of

Baghdad in a red zone. It was very dangerous. We had an alarm system that was supposed to go off when a bomb was headed our way, but it was broken. So that was another level of anxiety. There were bullet shells all over the ground and trash everywhere. Our commissary, the place we got food from, would run out of food very quickly since it was so small. So my mom would send me care packages, which temporarily brought me a little joy. That December, I experienced yet another curveball when I was diagnosed with cancer. I was exhausted all the time, but I didn't think much of it because, after all, I was in the middle of war. About a month later, I found a lump in my leg. I thought that maybe I'd pulled a muscle or torn a muscle off the bone. Despite my nonchalance about it, my mother was very concerned. Mostly to satisfy her, I went and got it checked out. I was the healthiest I'd ever been in my life, working out harder than some of the guys out there. It couldn't be anything too serious.

I was sent to Germany for testing, and we found out that the lump was a tumor. I was diagnosed with sarcoma, a rare type of cancer that grows in the bones and soft tissues. I remember calling my mom around nine in the morning to tell her and she just screamed. It crushed me to hurt her like that because I took pride in being the golden child—out of the way and never requiring much. She left her job and flew to D.C. to meet me at Walter Reed National Military Medical Center, where I'd been transferred. My husband (at the time) also came. Though he was physically present, he was mentally absent. He'd be on the phone at all hours of the day and night. He even flirted with some of the hospital staff. At this point, no one thought I'd survive. I recall the chaplain coming in my room nearly every day and asking me if I believed in God and if I lived an honest life...one that would get me through the pearly gates of heaven. I was constantly bombarded by questions; one question stuck out to me the most and it came from one of the nurses—she asked me if I was sure I wanted to leave him, my husband, in my will.

"What do you mean?" I asked her.

She responded, "If I were you, I wouldn't put him in the will."

See, everyone could see how absent he was and how unmoved he was about my condition except for me. I was in true denial and couldn't entertain the idea of the man I loved plotting to leave me. In addition to battling cancer, I was forced to deal with the reality of it all and heartbreak. Then one day he announced that he was moving to California for a modeling gig. Who in their right mind leaves someone who is possibly going to die any day? The answer to that question is a heartless person, that's who.

Alarms in my head and in my heart went off—I felt the seeds of heartbreak and war flowering inside my gut...again! I was still the girl who'd been left in Oregon by her mother, whose father suddenly passed away, and whose stepfather left the family for dead. I couldn't deal with possibly being abandoned by my husband. After all those years of not being able to trust, I finally dropped my guard and let someone in, and now he was about to leave me? I told him that as long as we stayed together, I'd support him. He agreed and I relaxed. Then I learned that he was moving to California to be with another woman. I was dying and he was leaving me—at a time when I needed him the most. That cut deep.

We talk a lot about trauma and triggers, but not how they compound. I'd still never gotten over my childhood pain, and now I had this to stack on top of that. Once again, I was furious about something that I could do nothing about. I felt like the seven-year-old Brandi, crying in the middle of the classroom. I wouldn't show the world my pain this time though. That was unacceptable. Grieving in public only results in ridicule and exile. So, I'd skip the embarrassment and the feelings of hopelessness and just leave. I no longer wanted to live because it didn't feel worth it. If at every turn, there would only be more struggle, what was the point in continuing? Life had proved that there was nothing to ever look forward to but more misery.

The divorce was my breaking point. Fortunately, I survived cancer, but a part of me was still dying inside. All the pieces of me were scattered everywhere, and I had no idea how to pick them up and put them back together. One of my resolutions, however, was to never trust another soul. I would never let my guard down again. If I was cold before, then I was subzero now. Whenever I felt people getting close to me, I'd ghost them. This worked for a while, abandoning others before they had the chance to abandon me. People would pour their hearts out to me with tears streaming down their face, and I'd be completely unmoved. We pick up coping mechanisms to get through painful ordeals, and, if we aren't careful, we'll carry these strategies with us long after they've served their purpose for us. That was my case.

Refusing to let anyone get close handicapped me. While I understood why I couldn't trust anyone, I didn't understand how that was holding me back. We need meaningful relationships with other people. Without it, we're isolated and unable to live whole, fulfilling lives. Trust is the foundation of a healthy relationship, but because I couldn't trust, I was cutting myself off from opportunities that would help me grow. It's a lot like being in a red zone at war. You should always be on alert and ready to move when necessary. Your fight-or-flight reactions are always turned on. As a result, you don't really have time to notice how damaging the lifestyle is. You're too busy trying to survive! Once you're back home, you must relearn how not to look at everything or everyone as a threat. You have to reacclimate to being safe.

Before I even went to war, I was already battling post-traumatic stress disorder. The things I'd gone through were not normal, but they were my norm. I'd grown accustomed to not knowing what to expect from one moment to the next. I'd also come to learn that I could only depend on myself and that it was in my best interest to forgo relationships and just focus on surviving. A person with a healthy perspective might've realized that what my parents did had nothing to do with me and that maybe I overlooked the red flags while dating because I was desperate to be seen and valued because of my childhood trauma. I didn't have a healthy perspective, though. I was operating from a place of hurt. So, there was no self-compassion. Instead, I went harder on myself and those around me...until I got tired of that, too.

I had countless friendships and dating situations come and go because of my coldness. Then one guy named Corey refused to let up. He put the proverbial mirror to my face and told me that I was getting in my own way. "Life could be so great, if you'd just put your walls down," he said.

I asked (probably more to myself than him), "But what if something bad happens?"

His response stuck with me: "But what if something great happens?"

That initiated my journey to healing my inner child. I started exploring why I went into every situation expecting the worst. I realized it was to safeguard myself from hurt or disappointment. If I predicted it, then I wouldn't be caught off guard. I dug through my prior years to see where that stemmed from, and there were ample aha moments.

I also started realizing how lonely I was as a result of keeping everyone out, and I was ready to get beyond that. If I didn't get my stuff together, this amazing soul named Corey would add to my list of what should've/could've/would've. I'd reached a place in my life where I didn't want to just survive anymore. I wanted to go beyond survival mode and experience what it felt like to love my life, to make myself proud, and to even help people who were going through what I'd already overcome. I had to acknowledge and release the baggage first though. So, in addition to self-inquiry, I also started meditating and reading books on mental health and personal development. I had to revisit all my past hurts, so I did a lot of overdue crying. I started opening myself up and sharing my story and learning to be okay with not knowing what was going to happen. The connection could amount to betrayal, yes, but it could also become something beautiful.

One situation at a time, I rewired my thinking to become more optimistic versus always just expecting the worst. Cynicism had (understandably) been my way of life for a long time, but it was no longer working for me. The transition wasn't easy, though. Being an asshole was my comfort zone. Practicing more grace and patience took time. Not only was I relearning how to show up for others, but I was doing so for myself as well. Figuring out what my triggers were and how to better respond when they presented themselves was another layer. Fortunately, Corey was there to support me through all of that. Ultimately, however, it was my responsibility to acknowledge my baggage and stop projecting my past experiences into my future. My mental health depended on my willingness and ability to do that.

Mental health dictates how we experience life. It determines how we think, how we feel, and how we show up in the world. Living in survival mode, in the red zone, will have you taking everything personally. Just because you had a bad day, a bad childhood, or a bad marriage doesn't mean you have to have a bad life. Until you acknowledge the flaw in your thinking and restructure it, you'll continue to wallow. Even if you've been diagnosed with a mental illness, you can still live a fulfilling life. Before my father passed away, he was being treated for schizophrenia. That treatment helped him steer clear of substance abuse. He developed a relationship with God and got a job and an apartment. He turned his life around, but I was never there to see it. Now my father is a beautiful memory told at my family gatherings and from the lips of my Aunt Julie. Had he been diagnosed and treated earlier on, it would've made a difference for him, for my sister and me, my mother, and everyone else who loved him (or otherwise consistently interacted with him). I would have had a dad, one that loved me. A dad who was patient and understood me. Access to quality health care, including mental health care, is critical to our society. It's a social problem, not just personal.

We all deserve to be healthy and whole in our minds, bodies, and spirits. Only then will you experience the good outweighing the bad. You'll be able to trust others because you can trust yourself. You can trust yourself because, time and time again, you've survived every obstacle that has come your way. You've grown to be resilient. And no one can shame you about anything you went through because you own your story. That ownership gives you power that no one can take from you. Equipped with that kind of power, you more effortlessly become the person you were destined to be with all the peace of mind you deserve to have. Don't let your outer or internal wars rob you of your joy or the person you want to be.

—**Brandi Benson**, author, cancer survivor, veteran

Those were just a few stories that I wanted to highlight here in my book. My mission doesn't begin or end with me alone. There are so many gifted storytellers in the world. I hope to illuminate thousands over my lifetime, sharing them with you so you can learn from them all. I firmly believe these few could change your life for the better. The space they hold in this book means as much to me as I hope it means to you.

CHAPTER 15

My Wish to Make Films and the Six Film Awards Won

The wish to make films for me began at thirteen years old when I saw *Ace Ventura: Pet Detective*, the greatest film ever to exist (LOL)! I saw what Jim Carrey accomplished in that film and I was hooked. For the longest time, I wanted to become an actor. I even performed in high school and college theater. Then I took film history and got really excited about the power of film. It was amazing to watch as films used storytelling to change minds, ideals, course correct cultures, and help people heal from trauma. Films help those watching escape their pain and struggle.

For others, especially documentaries and some major biopic narrative films like *Dallas Buyers Club*, there became a call to action after the film. Just look at the Dallas Buyers Club Law that went into effect because of the film and its makers. Shout out to Rachel Winters and Dorothy Canton for making such an important, life-changing movie. Films can be used to do great good in the world. I certainly hope all of mine accomplish such a truth. During this lengthy period in my life, a time where everything veered off track, my brain health was in shambles. I was coming apart at the seams. I was in and out of psych wards. I was on and off medications, and my brain was again broken. During that time, the thoughts and visions of being a filmmaker never died. I got a chance to get close to the process when I was invited to be a part of Eric Steel's famed film *The Bridge*. I knew right there that someday I would become an acclaimed documentary filmmaker. #LIFEGOALS, it all came true.

The six film awards we won for our collaborative film *Suicide: The Ripple Effect* were unexpected and at the same time amazing. Our first film out the gate won several international film awards including Best Film, Best Long Documentary, and Documentary of the Year. It was very fulfilling, all on our first film. The story we told expanded on my life journey while telling the broader story of global suicide prevention. It changed the trajectory of my life. It inspired my wife and I to start a small film production company 17th & Montgomery Productions. Today we create documentaries, short films, and a great deal of online viral media. My father said it best: "Kevin, you've come a long way from under the Golden Gate Bridge."

I co-directed and co-produced the film with a man named Greg Dicharry. He too has a bipolar disorder. We were just two bipolar kids who had dreams of making films. He'd done some music videos and a short film in the past, and I had trained in acting for the camera. We both had a vision. Well, two separate visions for the film, really. During the filmmaking process, we fought on many small details, but all of that aside, we could not have done it without each other. He and I each had our strengths and our shortfalls. Even so, we complemented each other well. The result was stellar. We had a great deal of help from our editor, scoring artist, and writer, Ryan Moser. Shout out to you, Ry Guy, without ya, our film wouldn't be what it is today.

My wife, Greg's ex-wife, our partners, and producers had a major hand in making this film such a great success. It's been seen so far by over two million people in twenty plus different countries. Thanks, Greg, for working with me to make history. Ours is one of the first documentaries to openly talk about suicide in a way that included effective messaging and encouraged help-seeking behaviors. It's something I'm quite proud of.

We traveled to six different countries during the making of the film: the United States, England, Canada, Ireland, Australia, and Japan. We captured stories from all over the globe. The experience was exceptional. We met two handfuls of

Australians and Americans who truly made the film special. Joe Williams was one of them. Joe is an Aboriginal Australian, a suicide prevention activist, an author, and a former professional sports star. Joe is a proud Wiradjuri First Nations Aboriginal born in Cowra, raised in Wagga Wagga, New South Wales, Australia. Joe played in the National Rugby League (similar to the NFL) for the South Sydney Rabbitohs, Penrith Panthers, and the Canterbury-Bankstown Bulldogs before he switched to professional boxing in 2009. Joe is a two-time BWF World Junior Welterweight champion and recently won the WBC Asia Continental title.

Joe was the Wagga Wagga Citizen of the Year in 2015 for his work within the community, mental health, and suicide prevention sectors. Joe is also a published author, contributing to the book *Transformation: Turning Tragedy to Triumph*. He even wrote his own book *The Enemy Within*. Joe now spends his time working to inspire youths and individuals through motivational speaking workshops run through his charity The Enemy Within. He has had his own battles, struggles, and setbacks, which culminated in his own suicide attempt in 2012. The Enemy Within Project shows a raw and honest side of Joe Williams, the boxer, former NRL player, father, and fiancé. Joe delves into the private pain and dealings with depression that drove him to the very brink. Joe talks adversity, dealing with struggle, resilience, improving your attitude by 1 percent, positive energy, and how small steps lead to something greater.

Joe lists becoming a father to five beautiful children as his greatest accomplishment. What a gift.

Others I met were Matt Runnalls, Ben Higgs, Lauren K. Breen, Sonia Higgins, Sam Webb, and Patrick Lawson. Their stories, messages of hope, and triumph over adversity set me on a path to glean from as many stories of resilience as I possibly could. I remain on that path. It's almost an obsession. Today, I search for the most incredible stories from all over the world; my hunger for such tales is insatiable. My goal is to publish these stories online for anyone and everyone to see. In doing so, we are continuing our mission to help save lives through storytelling.

The film made it into the Nice International Film Festival, the Woodstock Film Festival, the International Black Film Festival, the ReelAbilities Film Festival, and several others. We split the awards between us. What a journey. I am working on making a new film. A film that is an ode to Eric Steel's film *The Bridge*. Our new film is called *The Net*. It is an investigative and journalistic look at the eight fights that failed in raising the rail at the Golden Gate Bridge to stop suicides there forever, and the one fight that won. We go on this path with family who have lost loved ones to the GGB's lethal allure. We sit with the founders of the BridgeRail Foundation, the only organization that was solely dedicated to the raising of a suicide prevention net at the Golden Gate Bridge. (Now it is dedicated to raising nets and rails all over the country and the world.)

The conversations were incredible, powerful, meaningful, and moving to your core. Our film is rooted in its masterful cinematic visuals that can only leave the viewer in awe.

CHAPTER 16

The Tipping Point of Stevens-Johnson Syndrome

The near-death experience that overtook my life and my wife's life was unbearable. One of my medications had poisoned my insides. It was affecting my organs. My body became inflamed. Boils and bloody blisters covered me head to toe. No topical cream worked; doctors had to take me off all medications simultaneously because if they did not, I would die. It was terrifying. Yet again, I survived.

I was on the tipping point of Stevens-Johnson syndrome, a condition where your insides boil outside of you and you die an agonizing and painful death. When the doctors involved took me off all psych, asthma, pain, and allergy meds in one twenty-four-hour period, I had a forty-eight-hour withdrawal-based psychosis. My friends reading this now, know this: I saw the answers to the universe. I saw Jesus, Gandhi, Buddha, the king of Bhutan, three aliens, six aboriginal elders, and all my demons in what appeared to be physical form. Then I saw the aurora borealis in my room for the remaining twenty-four hours of that forty-eight-hour period coming off those pills. It was mind bending to say the least.

Let's get into it! Okay, so after I was rushed to the hospital for the burns that formed on my skin from head to toe, we headed home. We'd been in Philadelphia, where I was speaking at a large corporate event. We arrived in Atlanta then headed to our quaint apartment. I was a wreck! First appeared the demons, darkness personified. It wasn't my first run in with such visions, yet still I remained terrified. There were what seemed to be thousands of demons in our room. Margaret disappeared; all I saw was blood, guts, gore, and total horror. Those dastardly demons whispered horrible things in my ears, telling me again that I had to die by my hands. I was in a complete psychotic state, hallucinating beyond reproach. I could see the room I was in as if it were the true reality.

I looked at our cross on the wall and that's when it happened: Jesus himself came off the cross, turned to me, and said, "All will be all right; you will get through this. I promise."

I asked him directly, "Hey Jesus, how the hell (no pun intended) do I get rid of the demons?"

He replied without hesitation, "Simple, just tell them you love them. Kindness and compassion to all is the key."

So, I turned to the demons in front of me, and all around me, and I said, "Guys, I love ya, now get the fuck outta here!" From that moment, three men appeared before my eyes. First, the king of Bhutan—Bhutan, where they study gross national happiness.

He looked at me and said, "Kevin, just be happy! It's up to you. Let me introduce you to a friend of mine."

The king of Bhutan introduced me to Buddha, who said very swiftly, "Quit f&%^*@! whining and man up!" Buddha then introduced me to Gandhi.

Gandhi, floating cross-legged above me in his ceremonial garb, immediately revealed to me my greatest truth. He said in that wonderful soothing accent, "Oh Kevin, my boy, everything is going to be all right, just breathe. Just breathe."

Then appeared in several rows right above me forty busts of Jesus Christ, the long hair, the beards, and a crown of thorns above all their heads. They were of all different ethnicities and spoke in all kinds of languages. Somehow, I understood them all. "Kevin, you are going to be okay, I promise! Let me show you who brought me here..."

Out of thin air rose three aliens front and center. A green, a white, and a gray one. They said simultaneously as if talking from one hive mind, "Kevin, we brought Jesus here, let us show you who brought us."

The air in front of me became foggy almost smoky, gray, and cloudy even. The fog disappeared, and there emerged six aboriginal elders from Australia, who are literally (in real life) considered the first humans on the planet.

The aboriginal elders spoke in their native indigenous tongue, and I understood them; oh, what the brain can do when under an immeasurable amount of stress. They said to me quite clearly, "Kevin, you are broken, but we promise this is just the beginning. You will not die here and now. The pain you will experience from today through the next year will test you beyond your limits. You will want to end it all. You will want to die every moment of each day. You will not end it all. You will not take your life. That is not your destiny, that is not your fate. Kevin, you must be here tomorrow and every single day after that. You must be an example. We have faith in your survival. When you are overcome, read every book you come across, read it again, then never read it again. Gain worldly knowledge. Then you will be ready to teach the masses how to be resilient in the face of such unbearable pain. Your battle will be inescapable, but you will continue. You will forge on. We believe in your will. Always remember pain is universal. Pain is inevitable, Kevin. Suffering, however, is optional; it's a choice. Don't let suffering be your choice. Choose to fight your pain, battle your pain, live with your pain, and thrive despite of it."

CHAPTER 17

The Mania, the Mania, the Mania

The mania, the mania, the mania that Margaret and I dealt with after my forty-eight-hour withdrawal-based psychosis ended up lasting the better part of two and a half years. My doctors were so worried for me they told my wife I might be stuck in the mania forever. They even said it was causing injuries akin to brain damage. Margaret feared for my safety, well-being, future, and life. The mania had completely taken over every aspect of my life. I spoke a mile a minute. Rapid thoughts ran through my mind; ideas overwhelmed me constantly. I was not eating, I could not sleep, and every sleepless night just fueled my mania. As Yoda would say, "Superhuman, I am." I felt invincible. My workout routines were unchecked and out of control. I'd workout sixteen times a day for a total of three hours each day. Because I wasn't eating, I became completely gaunt. I was living with anorexia. I was almost in shock, constantly thinking and overthinking, planning grandiose unrealistic endeavors. I was out of control. My gauge for what was real was shattered, broken, and dismantled simultaneously.

The physical pain was intolerable and unrelenting. I never wanted to die when I jumped from the GGB; I only believed that

I *had* to—and those are two categorically different things. During this pain caused by a new medication and inflammation, it felt like knives and needles were piercing from my bones through my skin and across my entire body. I had bloody blisters and second-degree burns everywhere. I wanted to die every single day, all day long. Instead, I fought the pain. I learned something during this time about pain. I learned through my hallucinations that pain is inevitable, but suffering is optional. Cultures around the world, outside of the United States, have learned how to meditate physical, emotional, and mental pain away. Why can't we?

Back to the mania, I was so far gone, I began to behave like an outsider from my family. From Margaret. I told her I no longer loved anyone or anything. I told her I had no connection to her, my father, mother, adopted brother and sister, my biological brother and sister, or anyone I had ever cared for. My brain was dictating my actions; I was not in command of my own life. I compare it to being at the driver's seat of your car doing seventy miles per hour with no understanding, emotional connection, or care that you're in a forty-five-miles-per-hour zone. You are endangering all the people around you.

My dad could tell when I called him that I was completely unwell. He would say to me, "Kevin, are you taking your pills?"

The reality at the time, according to my doctors, was that I could not take pills until I got the burns and blistering under control. However, I simply told my dad a lie that would break the bond of trust I'd been rebuilding for over twenty years since my attempt off the Golden Gate Bridge. He knew I was lying when I said that I was still on meds; he could tell. He could always tell. This not only broke his trust of me, but it sent him back straight into the post-traumatic stress disorder that he developed from my attempt. It's taken a long time; he struggles daily with what I did. It caused real damage to his psyche, but we are on great terms. I call or text the man every day. People always say they have no regrets. Well, I do. I hurt a lot of family and friends during multiple manic episodes spanning over twenty-two years.

When you have that kind of effect on people, you need to take responsibility for the hurt you've caused. You have an obligation to make amends. Leave no stone unturned. Apologize to those you know you've hurt, ask for forgiveness, and remember to forgive yourself. Every one of us can be one thousand times greater than the worst thing we've ever done. I try to lead a life today filled with hope first, then purpose, then unconditional love for those who mean the world to me. When I'm in brain pain, I take stock of it, I hold gratitude for it, become resilient from it, and recognize that I am meant to be here until my natural end. When the suicidal ideations approach, I acknowledge them, fight them, work through them, ask for help, then I put all my efforts into getting to the root of the problem.

CHAPTER 18

Storytelling Saves Lives

Sharing stories has been a part of societal culture since the dawn of time. Every human who has ever existed tells or shares stories. Whether loud, vocal, mute, deaf, blind, or otherwise, we all find ways to share what we feel, what we've seen, and the pain we've experience. Stories and those who retell them have completely reshaped empires. Think of the art of filmmaking, the intricate tales told in modern video games, old novellas, history books, and theologians over the course of life itself. There is great lore in the art of storytelling. It is our greatest asset, and quite possibly our most important endeavor. If we did not share stories, how would we pass along the history of our ancestors to those we love, care about, and know here in the present day? If I draw breath, I will share my story.

Stories are twenty-two times more memorable than statistics or facts. When one shares a story, especially a harrowing and hopeful one, those listening or watching sync up with the person telling or sharing the story. Their brain's neural pathways mirror that of the storyteller. It's frickin' incredible. The hero's journey affects brains in a visceral way, and can actually change the listener's or viewer's brain for the better. When a particular story holds our attention for a long enough period, emotionally, we sync up with the character or characters of the story. Whether you are listening to a breathtaking podcast, reading a powerful book, or watching an exceptional movie, your brain, once hooked, feels the experience of what you are hearing or seeing. That's why you can almost feel the hits when Captain America is getting pummeled in a Marvel movie.

I have been lucky enough to share my story for over twenty-two years. The responses have been incredible. I have seen firsthand the effects of storytelling, and not just my own. Some years back, Margaret and I launched a speaker collective, The CNQR collective, as in *conquer* your pain. Every person on it had real life battles from hell, and they came out on the other side better for their lived experiences. Each of them was on their own hero's journey. Each of them was paving a path toward better brain health and well-being. Finally, each of them was working toward helping save the lives of those they spoke and speak to. Many of these collective members have gone on to start their own foundations, run programs in schools, make their own documentary films, or write their memoirs, and each has truly found success.

It's been amazing to watch them grow, change, and save lives forever with their life stories. I know their stories well, but every time I hear them, I'm moved to tears, then moved to action. They end up inspiring me. What a gift!

CHAPTER 19

Is Suicide Selfish?

Diane, my friend, could not relate to stories from people that hadn't lived it.

People told her that her brother-in-law's suicide was selfish. My story taught her that it wasn't. Her brother-in-law thought it would benefit others if he wasn't around. Dr. Thomas Joiner's books were the most helpful in Diane's healing from her unbelievable loss. On the day he died, Diane's brother-in-law put his wallet on his desk and took the chip out of his phone.

Friends would say, "But he was so happy right before!"

She determined that he was happy to finally end the pain. My situation was similar. I was elated that the pain was going to end. She needed to contact me to see what was going on with her experience. She found my contact info through social media, she reached out, and it helped her. This opened such a safe place for her and many others. "You have to talk to Kevin, 'cause he's the savior," she would tell friends who had lost loved ones or family who had mental illness. She was blown away by the way that I was so accessible. To her, it was amazing.

When her phone rings and she has no idea who's calling and it's someone who's in serious pain and needs her help, it keeps her going and is quite like one of my main purposes in life: helping people find hope. Even in our darkest moments, when we are planning to leave this world, we can always find a reason to stay. Even if someone is in such a dark, bad place—planning to use a gun, leap off a bridge, use a rope or pills—this is in no way a selfish act. They are not trying to hurt those they love. Once you realize someone's trying to take their life in such a violent way, there is no way it's a selfish act. You must realize how much of an awful place they had to be in to get to that point. We need to hold more compassion and empathy for those in that position, for those with severe brain pain. Those who died by suicide were hurting so terribly they didn't want to burden those who love them. Those who take their lives end up utilizing a dangerous kind of courage that leads to their demise.

For those who remain behind after a loved one's suicide, you may not be able to move on, but you can certainly stop asking the question *why?* It is an unanswerable question; instead, we must look to the living and move forward. For a person to be selfish, they can only be concerned with self and chiefly concerned with one's personal profit of pleasure, thus lacking any and all concern for others. Was the person you loved who died by suicide generally a selfish person? If not, how could they be selfish when they took their life?

Maybe believing that your loved one was selfish for dying by suicide makes it easier for you to cope with their death. When you look at how dark of a place someone needs to be in to take their life, it's truly a dangerous kind of horrible and misplaced courage. The kind of courage we need to prevent at all costs to save lives, to help people to always be here tomorrow.

CHAPTER 20

How Dwayne "The Rock" Johnson Helped Keep Me Here

It has been twenty-two years and some change since the day I should have died off of the Golden Gate Bridge. Twenty-two years of survival in the face of pain. Twenty-two years of finding hope in my darkest hours. Twenty-two years of people around me helping me stay here, and twenty-two years of lived experiences to help others do the same. I have a completely new lease on life, and it levels up every single year that passes. What a gift that I get to be alive, one I am most grateful for. I am thankful for everything I get to do, every place I get to go, and every single person I get to meet. This new lease on life won't last forever, but it will last until I perish naturally. I no longer fear death, but I know for a fact that I will never die by my hands.

I'm incredibly inspired by people who lay their pain bare, all on the line for the world to see. I am so moved by those who tell the story of their personal battles in life, how they found hope, and how they continue. Dwayne "The Rock" Johnson has had a massive effect on my personal well-being. His honesty about his mental health as such a proud and public figure has on many occasions moved me to tears and then helped me remain resilient. It has helped me on many occasions remain alive. I believe in giving people their flowers while they're still here. I hope one day to meet the man, the myth, the legend he is, shake his hand, and simply say, "Thank you, Dwayne 'The Rock' Johnson; you helped save my life." His words inspired me just like I hope my words in this book inspire you. People often ask me what I would have done differently. My answer today: not a thing. What will be will be; what has been made me the man I am today. Everything happens for a reason. I'm just so glad I survived.

My message to others, though, one more time so you don't forget! Please don't learn the hard way like I did. Choose life before you try an attempt on yours and ask, plead, and beg for help instead of attempting at all. If you have related to anything I've put down here, please consider finding someone willing to empathize and ask for help. You deserve it. You are worthy, you do matter, you are important, and I know I don't know you, but you are important to me. If no one else says it today (because I recognize a lot of you out there are growing up in broken and abusive homes) I love you and I want you to stay. If in crisis, immediately dial 988 or text CNQR to 741741 for trained crisis counselors. Stay safe, do the hard work to heal, and whatever you do, always #BEHERETOMORROW.

The Relationship that Saved My Life— Over and Over and Over Again

Margaret Hines, my beautiful bride, has saved my life above all else. She has saved my life on more times than I can count on my hands and feet. She continues to save my life every day. She does this by being there in every moment and in the present. She guides me in life, in love, and in business. My Margaret makes every single day worthwhile. Our love is a miracle and absolutely the greatest gift God has ever given me. We love each other unconditionally, passionately, and emotionally. We tell each other everything and that is how we overcome any obstacles found in our way.

Thank you, my love, for inspiring me to do better, be better, and to grow as a person each day. I don't write this epilogue to boast about my love life. I write it to share that even if you are in a world of pain today, it does not mean you won't get to have that beautiful tomorrow, but you must be here to get there in the first place. Just because you struggle today doesn't mean you will struggle tomorrow.

Hard work plus hope equals healing and recovery from brain pain. You can overcome, you can achieve, you can find enormous success. Not necessarily monetary success, but life skill success, the success of being in the moment no matter the pain you might be experiencing.

Could total bliss be a reality for you? I think yes; I think finding total bliss is completely up to you. Finding and creating a life worth living, that reality is in your hands. Take responsibility for your mental well-being. You can do this, I believe in you, I believe in your ability to be well. I'm here for moral support; find me at @KevinHinesStory across all socials. Reach out. If I can, I'll reach back. I can't reach everyone, but I can try to send a message or make a public post on socials that affects you in a positive way. #KeepOnKeepinOn, remember #HopeHelpsHeal, and whatever the heck you do #BeHereTomorrow and every single day after that. You are loved, you are valued, you are worthy, and you matter. You matter to me. And if no one else says it today, I love ya and I want you to please stay.

Contributors

Patrick (Pat) Lawson is a husband, father, son, and brother. However, in February of 2015, Pat had another item to add to his list… Suicide Attempt survivor.

In February 2015, Pat was what he describes as "at the lowest point I have ever been" to a point where ending his life felt like the only answer to every question running around his head.

Thankfully, that day didn't turn out the way he had (unwillingly) planned and now, Pat uses his lived experience to help educate the people all around the globe about the effect Mental Illness and suicidal ideation can have on a person and different ways to help manage your daily struggles.

In his talks, Pat speaks of battling his demons, the day that changed his life, the importance of educating yourself, what living with BPD (Borderline Personality Disorder) can look like, self-care and self-awareness, and so much more.

Pat doesn't claim to have "all the answers," however, he loves sharing his story to help answer some of the wider asked questions surrounding daily battles and how to help manage your illness to allow yourself to live a better life.

@PatLawson_mh

Joe Williams is a Wiradjuri/Wolgalu First Nations Aboriginal man born in Cowra, raised in Wagga NSW having lived a fifteen-year span as a professional sports person. Joe played in the National Rugby League for South Sydney Rabbitohs, Penrith Panthers, and Canterbury Bulldogs before switching to professional Boxing in 2009. As a boxer, Joe was a two-time World Boxing Federation (WBF) World Junior Welterweight champion and also won the World Boxing Council (WBC) Asia Continental title.

Although forging a successful professional sporting career, Joe battled the majority of his life with suicidal ideation and Bipolar Disorder. After a suicide attempt in 2012, Joe felt his purpose was to help people who struggle with mental health and wellbeing, and he founded the organization The Enemy Within.

Since founding The Enemy Within in 2014, Joe has delivered wellbeing & trauma recovery programs to hundreds of communities across Australia, New Zealand, and the USA.

The Enemy Within aims to alleviate the mental and traumatic distress of individuals from all pockets of community.

Joe was also named as a finalist for the Courage Award in the 2017 National Indigenous Human Rights Awards, and in 2018, he was awarded the Suicide Prevention Australia Life Award. In 2019, Joe was awarded Australia's highest honor in the mental health field as a co-winner of the National Mental Health Prize.

Joe's autobiography, *Defying The Enemy Within*, was released in 2018.

Facebook: The Enemy Within: Suicide Prevention, Trauma Recovery & Wellbeing Education
Instagram: @joewilliams_tew
Twitter: @joewilliams_tew

 **Brandi Benson** was diagnosed with terminal cancer in 2009 while serving in Iraq with the U.S. Army. She was given an eight to twelve-month life expectancy with a 15 percent chance of surviving. Since then, Brandi has devoted her life to advocating for cancer patients and survivors, as well as veterans facing similar diagnoses, and she uses her platform to encourage others not to give up on themselves by sharing her remarkable story of hope, resiliency, and the art of rebelling against those who do not believe in miracles.

As a result, she's devoted her life to raising awareness about rare illnesses and the importance of physical and mental recovery and has made it her mission to provide an effective blueprint of strategies and tasks that survivors, their loved ones, and anyone struggling with an "enemy" in whatever form can use to take charge of their healing and wellness.

Brandi is the author of the book, *The Enemy Inside Me*, an Iraqi War Veteran (Operation Enduring Freedom), an award recipient from the Sarcoma Foundation of America, and best known for her signature talk *"There Are Miracles Every Day, Why Can't You Be One?"*

During Brandi's engagements, she emphasizes the importance of a strong support system, the beauty of vulnerability, how to integrate back into the workplace after an illness (cancer), and changing the survivorship narrative.

Instagram: BrandiL.Benson
Facebook: Brandi L. Benson
Twitter: Brandi L. Benson
TikTok: Brandi L. Benson

Ashley Hunt, CEO and founder of Pancea Health is a serial entrepreneur, author, advocate, kinesiologist, and corrective and orthopedic exercise specialist. With ten years of experience working in musculoskeletal injury prevention and recovery, Ashley has founded multiple musculoskeletal care companies and is on a mission to help millions of people around the world know how to manage their daily health anytime, anywhere. In addition to her digital health company, Ashley is an advocate for anti-sexual violence and protecting victims of abuse. She has hosted fundraisers for Bay Area Women Against Rape, spoken at multiple universities, and is a co-author of *The Art of Being Broken*. Ashley's passion in advocacy comes from her own personal experience and she hopes that sharing her story will help others know that healing is possible.

@ashleyhunt_2

@Pancea.Health

https://www.pancea.ai/

@BoonDockMom

Dayna Atkins Whitmer has served as a board member for the BridgeRail Foundation since 2008, following the disappearance of her youngest son, Matthew, in November 2007. Without recovery of his body, he remains a missing person and suspected suicide from the Golden Gate Bridge.

Through the BridgeRail Foundation, she and her husband, Mark, have spoken out about their loss locally, at state and federal levels, and internationally. They are strong advocates for suicide prevention and mental health awareness, including volunteering with the American Foundation of Suicide Prevention and National Alliance on Mental Illness.

Dayna served as the supervisor for the Neurology and Sleep clinical labs at a Veteran's Administration health care facility for over thirty years. She is a co-author with Dr. David L. Woods of the peer-reviewed article, "Analysis of the Cost Effectiveness of a Suicide Barrier on the Golden Gate Bridge" published 2013 in *Crisis*, the journal of the Crisis Intervention and Suicide Prevention. doi.org/10.1027/0227-5910/a000179

Photo by Louise Wright

Jas Rawlinson is a best-selling author, award-nominated book coach, and resilience speaker who specializes in stories that change lives. Combining her lived experience as a domestic violence survivor with her BA in creative writing and psychology, she has helped close to thirty writers to go from "idea" to "published" in the past four years, and has impacted hundreds of thousands of lives through global media outlets, including *Business Insider*, *Yahoo Finance*, news.com.au, and *Authority Magazine*. She is also the founder of Brisbane's first domestic violence memorial and an anti-human trafficking ambassador. Endorsed by high-profile names including Kevin Hines, Lifeline, and LIVIN, Jas speaks regularly on issues such as domestic violence and suicide prevention, and in 2023, she starred on the award-winning TV series *Adventure All Stars* as part of her mission to end child trafficking. Above all, Jas believes that everyone has a story with the power to inspire, impact, and change lives.

You can connect with her on Instagram @jas_rawlinson or at https://jasrawlinson.com.

Lindsey Dunbar is lives in Colorado with her amazing husband, Matt, and their two dogs, Kirra and Leo. She works as a therapist, discovering her true calling after working in the public health sector for several years around community mental health, stigma reduction, and suicide prevention as well as going through months of grief counseling for multiple pregnancy losses. Lindsey graduated with her second master's degree in clinical mental health counseling from University of Phoenix in 2022. She earned her first master's degree in public health sciences and worksite wellness from University of West Florida in 2016 and her bachelor's degree in exercise science and health promotion from Colorado State University (CSU) Pueblo in 2014. Lindsey was also a mentor for several months through Miscarriage Matters, Inc., helping women who have suffered their own losses across the country process, cope, and grieve their pregnancy and/or infant losses. Having gone through five consecutive miscarriages herself, Lindsey became very passionate about this topic. Lindsey continues to help people of all ages work through their own struggles and strive to obtain and maintain positive mental health. Dealing with anxiety herself since she was about eight years old, she also continues down the path of healing mentally and emotionally. In her spare time, she loves spending time with Matt, their dogs, and other family members, hiking, running, doing yoga, being out in nature, playing piano, binge watching favorite shows over and over, and traveling!

@LoveAndLumos_8314

About the Author

Kevin Hines is a storyteller at heart. He is a bestselling author, global public speaker, and award-winning documentary filmmaker. In 2000, Kevin attempted to take his life by jumping off the Golden Gate Bridge. Many factors contributed to his miraculous survival, including a sea lion that kept him afloat until the coast guard arrived. Kevin now travels the world sharing his story of hope, healing, and recovery while teaching people of all ages the art of wellness and the ability to survive pain with true resilience. Currently, Kevin is in pre-production of a feature film about his life, as well as his new docuseries *The Journey*, and is working on a comic book version of his life in cosmic and supernatural form called *Hope Dealers*. His fight has been long and arduous, but he is determined to remain committed to life until its natural end. His motto: #BeHereTomorrow and every day after that.